FINDING STRENGTH IN THE DARK

A STORY OF HOPE, LOVE, FAITH AND, HOT PINK MARY JANES

ANNETTE PEARSON

First published by Ultimate World Publishing 2020
Copyright © 2020 Annette Pearson

ISBN

Paperback: 978-1-922497-24-6
Ebook: 978-1-922497-25-3

Cover design: Ultimate World Publishing
Layout and typesetting: Ultimate World Publishing
Editor: Marnae Kelley

Ultimate World Publishing
Diamond Creek,
Victoria Australia 3089
www.writeabook.com.au

DEDICATION

*I dedicate this book to all of the women
who feel they have lost their strength.*

To the women who feel in the dark.

You are NOT alone!

FOREWORD

WRITTEN BY
FAITH PEARSON, AGE 10

Dear Mommy,

You are the best mommy I could ever have or anyone could ever have. I love you so much and you are the best. I know I want to be a trauma surgeon when I grow up, but if I'm being honest, the thing I most want to do is be like you. You're caring, loving, sweet, and you can handle so many things at once. You care about everyone so much. You always have Daddy's and my best interests at heart. I think it's amazing that you wrote this book. I love you so much—more than I could ever love anything or anyone in the world.

Love,
Foofy

INTRODUCTION

BY TOM PEARSON

When Annette and I started talking on a dating site, I did not realize my life was about to change forever. We would talk for hours at night, send messages back and forth, and exchange emails constantly. I learned so much about her during those long talks, building the groundwork that would make us best friends and lead to our falling in love. During those nights spent talking, I began to get an idea of the adversity Annette had been through and the inner strength and peace she had. Little did I know, I had just seen the tip of the iceberg.

You are about to read the story of the strongest woman I have ever known, and I am lucky to call her my wife, my love, and my best friend. She has overcome heartbreaks, physical pain, and adversity enough to grind anyone down, yet she always finds the strength to pick herself back up and keep going. It is not how a person acts when life is going well that tells you who they are. It is how they react when life is hard and everything is falling apart around them that tells their true story. Even when life events have pulled her to her lowest, Annette has always been able to find the strength to come back stronger.

Annette has been the strength that has carried our family forward. She and I have dealt with life changes, family stresses, a move across the country, and loss of loved ones and babies. It is through Annette's love and strength that our family has pushed through the darkness and tough times and come out the other side stronger. Annette's strength, peace, and love taught me how to love again after a tough divorce that I thought had wiped the ability to love out of me. Her inner strength, ability to think of others before herself, and love for those around her inspires and strengthens me daily. I hope this story of how she finds her strength will help you find your own strength in the dark and move forward to your light.

DISCLAIMER

I am not a medical professional. This is my story and in no way is it meant to provide medical advice nor invoke doubt or fear nor become your story. Should you have any questions or concerns related to the topics discussed in this book, please contact your physician.

CONTENTS

CHAPTER 1

THE MANSION AND ME

There was a point in my life where I had a mansion in Beverly Hills, a Corvette, a BMW, a Class A motorhome, and the most beautiful clothes. I had the ultimate Barbie collection. I fantasized about Barbie's life being my life. Barbie had it all: she had a brilliant future with her many trades, gorgeous tall husbands (and multiple boyfriends, oops...do you think one of the Kens knew?), and thousands of babies, and her prettiest shoes cost only 50¢. It was always a toss-up of who had the better life, Barbie or Marcia Brady, but Marcia had a complex about herself ("Marcia, Marcia, Marcia"). Barbie's life, in my opinion, was definitely the best, and I just knew I would grow up to be like Barbie. All I had to do to make it happen was have someone open the magical pink box and throw the glitter for me.

I was born in 1975 in the heart of the Valley, Tarzana, California (yes, I AM a Valley Girl). My mother, Ruth, was a key punch operator and my father, Howard, a mechanic. My father had a hard time holding jobs due to his learning disabilities. He had what we now know as dyslexia, but to his employers, he couldn't read and they called him "stupid," and he was anything but stupid; he was smart and very talented. The financial and emotional strain began to pull at my parents' marriage, and they separated when I was three and divorced at four. My parents tried to protect me from the pains of divorce, but no matter how much glitter they threw at it, Dad had moved into a one-room apartment, Mom was either crying or working, and Grandma was making spaghetti with ketchup.

Backstory: Grandma Beatrice was an amazing cook. However, to Beatrice, spaghetti was made by boiling the noodles, placing the bowl on the table and setting a bottle of ketchup next to it. Mom grew up knowing this as spaghetti but also knowing she didn't like spaghetti very much. Upon returning from their honeymoon, Dad left the house one day for work and asked my Mom to please make spaghetti for dinner. Dad returned home from a long day to a bowl of noodles and a bottle of ketchup. Dad, being from New York, appreciated a good bowl of spaghetti and this would just not do. Mom learned his family's recipe and never again served ketchup with pasta.

With Mom and Dad divorced, Mom was working three jobs to make ends meet. This meant that after I graduated from before-and-after-school care (actually, got kicked out for playing "house" with a boy) in the third grade, I was responsible for getting myself to and from school, breakfast in the morning, snack in the afternoon, homework done, and the dishwasher started before Mom got home. This new-found responsibility taught me a love for education, and shortly after, I became a school teacher. I taught the third through fifth grades in a one-room "school." I had a very large class. The students were quiet, attentive, and pleasant, but they never finished their school work, tests, and homework. I had to send the students (my stuffed animals), to the principal's office daily. I was also the principal, and the lessons I taught were, coincidently, my homework. As the principal, when needed, I wouldn't hesitate to break out the dunce hat and put them in the corner. I was also successfully able to divide my time between teaching and selling plastic dream houses in Beverly Hills, and I always won the negotiation. Between blonde plastic dolls and stuffed animals, I had it all, and I never felt that I had anything less.

This new responsibility showed me a new love for being a caretaker. Even though I had to keep my kid reputation and be stubborn and refuse, I honestly did not mind doing this work around the house because I grew to love the responsibility of "taking care" of a house. My dreams shifted to the dream of how Barbie did it all:

work many dream jobs, run the house and camping trips, and take care of thousands of babies plus her sister Skipper, all while Ken just came home for dinner and a new change of clothes. I dreamt of being a mom, a wife, taking care of my family, and doing it all while holding down my dream job, and if possible, a pink house.

As a child I became a frequent flyer. After my parents divorced and we moved, I travelled cross country on my own over school breaks and to San Francisco to visit family. After traveling on airplanes, I fell in love with the travel industry, and upon learning that there was a flight attendant Barbie, my dream job became a flight attendant. Since I was in my "boys are icky" stage, I had decided I would have 60+ children by immaculate conception or rubbing elbows and that my mom would care for them on my travel days. I had written out my travel schedule: I would travel around the world and return home to my children in 24 hours and then be home the remainder of the week with my mom taking care of the children during my 24 hours away. My mom wasn't too keen on the idea, and I was angry because she wasn't supporting my dreams. One day, in the heat of a childhood dramatic moment, my mom bestowed the "blessing" on me: "I hope one day you have kids JUST like you," she said as I was sent off to my room, grounded. I really didn't understand why she was both praising and grounding me at the same time.

Backstory: When I was eight, the boy next door decided, randomly, that he wanted a kiss. I did not want to kiss; my heart was pledged to another boy. I ran, he chased, I ran around a tree, he chased around a tree, I fell into the tree and chipped my front tooth. With a bloody mouth, I turned to the boy and offered a kiss, and the boy ran away. This was the start of my boys are icky phase. A few days later, he walked by me on the way to school, and while he was rushing past me, we somehow rubbed elbows. I was so worried that I would end up pregnant! My first lesson about the birds and the bees was when my dad told me that "pregnancy happens when a man and woman rub elbows." He said, "After the act of rubbing elbows, the man carries the babies in his armpit, and that is the reason babies smell." From that point on and until my next birds and the bees discussion, I covered my elbow and kept it tucked by my side. Years later my dad realized that I was old enough for the real lesson and said, "Here is what you need to know: the birds go chirp and the bees go buzz." I wondered if the lesson was that I should stay away from birds and bees. My last lesson came from my first gynecological visit after my dad passed away: "You know... sperm is so strong that you can get pregnant even through jeans or just by sitting on a toilet." As puberty continued, I figured it out on my own and then again in Sophomore Year when the health teacher spent weeks going over the human reproductive system.

Once I realized I wanted a family, at age eight, it seemed that every action, decision, whatever, kept the dream in my heart. At age eight, I had the next billion decades planned out. My life would become Barbie's, easy. In my mind I have been writing this book for as long as I remember. Maybe not this version or this topic, but I always dreamed that my life would be so wonderful that someone would write a book about me.

I am in project management by day, and shortly into my marriage, my husband, Tom, still didn't understand how my brain worked. Then one day we were iced in (gotta love a good Southern ice storm), and we were both working from home. I was tasked with writing a risk plan because that is one of the main responsibilities of a project manager, to plan for and respond to risks. In a matter of 12 hours I cranked out a 50-page plan that provided a response to earthquakes, snow storms, hurricanes, lost equipment, massive illness in the office, etc. Suddenly he got me—my brain made sense to him. I am programmed to think of the worst that can happen and plan every detail to "fix it."

Fun Fact: Tom and I took his kids, my step kids, to Disney World for a vacation. This would be the first big vacation as a family unit of four and my first time at Disney World (I am a Disneyland girl). I prepared a three-inch binder of itineraries, coupons, budgets, maps, and packing lists. Tom discovered my binder and threw it out, saying "project manager, STOP!"

Years later while looking at strollers, Tom went into full panic about all the stroller options and said, "You, you're the planner, where's your binder, what's the plan for the stroller?" I was so happy to say, "No, I do not have a plan because you never said project manager, GO!"

Now as an author I am nervous about telling my reality to the world. You see, I started writing in my journal in January, after my daughter, MaryGrace Hope, was born asleep. I was sharing some of my journal with my grief support group, and the facilitator told me my writing was beautiful and she felt that I had a message of hope, love, and faith for women whose hearts were in dark places, like mine. After much prayer, I felt called to share my story, not only to help myself heal and work through my grief but also to be a source of help and caring for women, regardless of their story.

So much of my life I have felt alone, abandoned, and lost within myself. Life was not like I planned. My father died when I was 12 from testicular cancer, which had spread to his brain, I was in a physically, sexually, and two emotionally abusive relationships, I had been at my financial breaking point multiple times, moved across the country three times, married a man with a complicated past, had a total knee replacement, sepsis, two major auto accidents, a crazy infertility journey, six miscarriages, and, in January of 2020, I was done. By time COVID hit, my light was completely out. I had nothing left to give. My reality was not at all what I planned, and I couldn't make the plan work.

Did you notice what I said? I couldn't. And in all of that I did not say, I SURVIVED! I write this book as a survivor that lives both inside and outside of darkness. I write this book to tell you about my dimmer switch, the same dimmer switch you have. I write this book because I have learned that I control the darkness, and God

7

controls the light. After a lifetime of ups and downs, pain, regret, sadness, grief, disappointment, etc. I have learned to give myself credit for getting up each day, putting one foot on the floor, then another, standing up, walking to the bathroom, peeing, washing my face, pulling on my big girl panties, and facing the day.

I promised I would be real, right? So, here is my truth. After signing with my wonderful publisher, I actually felt like scrapping this book altogether. Who am I to speak about finding the light and finding the strength when there are days when all I can do is get through one breath at a time. I am not an expert. What could I possibly tell you about my dreams, my realities, and how I found my strength? Then I realized, that is the answer. I don't have the answer. I can't "fix it" and once I realized I couldn't "fix it" I just lived life, I found my inner badass, and I started to turn on the light, and when I was able to open my eyes and sit tall, then...I knew I had something to tell you.

> *"Someone once asked me how I hold my head*
> *up high after all I've been through.*
> *I said, because no matter what, I am a survivor, not a victim."*
> *~ Patricia Buckley*

I have survived crisis, grief, abuse, trauma, and tragedy many times, and people are always asking me, "How did you do it, how did you keep going?" And my response, "I don't know, I guess I just had to."

Have you ever experienced laughter that comes from deep down inside, the kind of laughter that makes you feel like you have to pee or your eyes are watering, or both? If you did, how did you feel after you laughed that hard? When I laugh this hard, my entire body engages and I release all of my tensions and I breathe. I don't laugh to avoid uncomfortable situations or conversations; for me laughter is a necessity in my life. Laughter is my meditation, laughter heals my soul and laughter signals my body to tell my heart, "We

THE MANSION AND ME

are going to be okay...we got this." So please, laugh throughout this book. I did while writing it, and I laughed as life happened, too.

I found my strength in the dark when I decided I wanted to laugh and allowed myself to do so. I found my strength when I opened my heart to trust. I found my strength when I accepted, I am a survivor, not a victim. I found my strength in the dark when I was able and ready to say, "Enough!" Whether it's a relationship, a feeling, or a bad pair of shoes, I need to be my own advocate because there is no better person to represent what I need than me.

CHAPTER 2

TEENAGE LOVE, VILLAINS, AND SUPERHEROES

When I was 13, I met my hero. Literally, my hero. Out of nowhere, he came running from around the corner, wearing an overshirt long enough to be a cape, holding his jacket like it was a cape, and he was flying. He stopped right at me and said, "Hi, my name is Andy, how can I save you, today?" He didn't save me that particular day. However, he became one of my most treasured friends, and many years later, he did save my life. I didn't realize at the time the impact he would have on me. I just remember he made me laugh, he made me laugh until I peed, he was my meditation, he was my "big brother" (not by blood), and he was my protector. Andy stood over six feet tall and loved Superman, so much so that he got a large "S" tattooed over his heart. Andy introduced me to Viking graveyards, hiking, and parental negotiations, and he also taught me to laugh at life. Andy introduced me to my first dramatic romance, and he affectionately called me "Fishing Tackle" because "A – Net" is something you use to catch fish. This nickname (along with Netsy) is still used today.

My friend Andy introduced me to the love of my teen'ish life. When I was 13 and in eighth grade, he was 17 and a junior in high school. My mom mostly approved of this budding relationship, though, because he was a band geek, played the tuba, wore braces and thick glasses, and was recovering from a broken jaw. We first met on a typical teenage date at the mall. That first moment I saw him, my mind took me to this hottie walking out of a red sportscar and striking a sexy pose; he was Jake and I was Samantha, and this was *Sixteen Candles*. *Sixteen Candles* was one of my favorite movies, I was in love before he even spoke. I refer to him as Jake, since he was my imaginary but real person. My Jake!

We had an amazing summer together, much better than Sandy and Danny did in *Grease*. I actually think they would have been jealous. Jake was a lifeguard at our pool, and I was the lifeguard's girlfriend. I would sun myself on his shifts, and he would get to see me in my bathing suit. I wish I could say we did other things besides hang out at the pool, but he had to work all the time and had no money, I think he was paying his dad for the 100th time for denting the Mustang.

Disclaimer: In exchange for Jake's permission to include our story, I was told I had to properly identify the Mustang (boys and their toys), so here goes: The Mustang was a 1968 red Fastback with black interior, a 302 engine, c4 auto trans, and 205/75r14 tires, which he knows because of all the tires he burned through and had to replace. Oh, and he does not know the gas mileage because he didn't care; his dad was paying for the gas (whatever all this means, but one thing I can check off my list).

Freshman Year in HS was Jake's Senior Year, and we were as much in love as a (newer) 14 and 17-year-old could be. He was the tuba player; I was the mallard freshman. We shared a locker with Andy, and Jake let me have the majority of his shelf. He walked me to all my classes, we wrote each other notes during classes, and eventually he gave me his varsity jacket from band and class ring. We were the 'IT' couple (as least in my dramatic teenage mind).

Homecoming was magical, and my big hair was on point! That night he gifted me with a gold necklace, which said, "I will never stop loving you." In my dramatic teenage brain, we were now engaged. We would become that high school sweetheart love story that we see on the crying channels.

Jake told me that he wouldn't be able to stay faithful to me in college if he left as a virgin; one night, with his parents out of the house, he snuck me in and with "Pump Up the Jam" (1989 by Technotronic) playing in the background, we attempted to take care of "business." we were so close, and then his mom walked in on us. BUSTED! Jake went to sleep that night still a virgin, and I went to sleep wondering if that actually counted. His parents and my mom decided that it was time for us to stop seeing each other, *and* we were both grounded. Neither of these posed a problem because we would just continue to see each other behind their backs. I mean, it would be a challenge, but every good love story has its conflict and this was ours. Let's be real, we shared a locker, lunch, and study hour, he still walked me to classes, I still had his jacket and ring. We were "living together" and "still engaged." Our story was a modern-day Romeo and Juliet, except we didn't die and our deaths did not reconcile our families. We did, however,

13

escape to a secret night in downtown Chicago, and I became the greatest of friends with his mom.

Shortly after, he cheated on me. The pressure of being kept apart was just too much. I forgave Jake because I loved him that much and I had already planned out our life of marriage, children, the yellow house, the white picket fence complete with a golden retriever (Ricky) and cocker spaniel (Lucy). Eventually, Jake broke up with me and broke my heart at the same time.

This story is important to tell as we are an example of overcoming the past, forgiveness, and moving forward. My grandma died in 2012. At the funeral, I felt a tap on my shoulder, and when I turned around, there was Jake! I hadn't seen Jake since 2003, yet he saw the news of my grandmother's passing on Facebook and remembered how close my grandmother and I were and drove several hours to be at the funeral and support me.

Today, we have a very strong friendship. In fact, I would consider Jake to be one of my best friends. Jake and my husband, Tom, are good friends and pick on me together. In fact, Tom and I both agree, Jake is someone we both trust to take care of our daughter if we couldn't. Weird, right!

After Jake and I broke up it seemed that I only let the bums into my life, and what I realize now is I was blocking my heart from feeling hurt, from feeling life, and from taking a chance on feeling happy.

In high school I decided that my future was in medicine, more specifically trauma. My senior year of HS, I joined the Future Health and Home Makers of America (FHA) co-op program. My goal was mainly to get out of school by 11 a.m. so I could take a nap before running off to sell shoes. My teacher, who I still keep in touch with to this day, asked me to participate in an FHA competition, and of course my first response was "What's in it for me?" The response:

"You get to miss school and work for the competition." Perfect! I was signed up, within minutes, to present in the illustrated speech category. My topic, child abuse and neglect. High school was four years of hell in halls, for me, and my real reasons for accepting the teacher's offer were 1) to get out of school as much as possible, 2) to hang out with other people, and 3) because I desperately needed to do something memorable in high school.

The Results!

- Local competition: First place, no way, seriously, how could this be?
- Regional: First place, no way, seriously? Me? How could this be?
- State: First place, no way, seriously? ME?? How could this be?
- Nationals: Second place, with makeup spilled all over my dress, and yes way!

"The happiness of your life depends on the quality of your thoughts." ~ Marcus Aurelius

I moved out of Mom's house at 19 because I was 19 and refused to follow her rules. I was ready to be on my own. As I left Mom's house abruptly, she reminded me that her front door was not revolving and encouraged me to make my decision with intention, not emotion. Still, I was 19 and in my 19-year-old brain, I knew it all and she knew nothing. I was enrolled in the nursing program of our local community college and was working full time at the local hospital as a critical care/ER tech. I loved my job; it fulfilled my need to care for people.

Fun Fact: While in my phlebotomy rotation we had to be able to draw on ourselves before we were set loose to the patients. We also had to be able to draw in the dark (because phlebots do it best in the dark). After successfully passing each of these challenges, it was time for clinicals. I walked into one man's room and said,

"Hi, I am Annette, I am here from the lab and need to draw some blood." The man responded, "If you stick a needle in my arm, I am going to roll over and die."

I reassured him and then proceeded to prepare for the blood draw, and when I put the needle in his vein, he coded. I quickly started CPR, and long story short, he died. From that minute on the joke was on me. "Don't let Annette draw your blood, she will scare you to death."

A few months later I met the newest love of my life. This new beau moved in within weeks and I had my "someone to take care of" and we were engaged a week later. We were moving full steam ahead. I quit my job because the hours didn't work for our relationship, and I also needed a higher-paying job since he "lost his job" a lot.

I was getting married and we would have a family. My apartment was too small for us, so I broke my lease and we moved across town to something bigger and more fitting for an engaged couple. The (now) fiancé would find himself constantly between jobs, and I found myself further and further away from my dreams. It still didn't matter; I had a fiancé and my own family. Six months into our engagement, I sold all my furniture and bought all new things, at his request, including a car, and another car, and another. We were as happy as he thought we should be.

I remember, like it was yesterday, the first time I started to feel like I was nothing and he was the only man that would have me...the night he told me during relations, "Annette, you're fat, you're ugly, and you need to count your blessings I want you." This continued for the entire duration (of six minutes). I felt dirty, unworthy, and unloved. I wasn't able to have relations with him, but I also wasn't given a choice; he was going to take what he wanted when he wanted and how he wanted it and would continue to put me down for the duration (of six minutes).

One night he told me he would be working late and stopping at his parents' on his way home. I "happily" sat at home, planning our wedding, while on the phone with another of his exes that would be a bridesmaid, and then went to bed. He came home, got into bed, pushed me off the bed, and fell asleep. I couldn't go back to sleep, so I went into the other room to watch TV. He left his clothes all over the apartment, and while I picked up his pants, a receipt fell out of his pocket. He had not been working. He wasn't at his parents'. He was at a fancy hotel using my credit card. I woke him up to confront him. I was done. That was the first time he hit me, and while he was using his fist on me, he was screaming at me that it was my fault he had to cheat because I wasn't fulfilling his needs, that he had to close his eyes when he was with me because I was so ugly and he needed a real woman for a night. I am nearly confident that I had a concussion. I woke up on the floor. I had a black eye, a massive headache, and a bruise on my stomach.

My fiancé was very attentive and loving for quite a while, and I was hopeful that phase of our lives was in the past. We moved forward even more in love and committed to each other. To make this happen, I made sure the house was always clean, laundry done, dinner on the table, and I was available whenever he wanted. I bought him a computer, another new car, whatever he needed to love me. Life was the perfect glitter for the next six months as long as I was the perfect fiancé.

We made a baby. I was late and didn't think anything of it, until I did. I couldn't wait to tell my fiancé; he wanted a family just as much as I did. I pictured us running off and eloping so we could be married before we told anyone. We would have our happily ever after. I didn't know that that day, he lost his job. I planned the perfect evening. I was so excited and just kept cuddling my stomach. He came home and I couldn't help but blurt out, "We're having a baby. I am pregnant." I never saw it coming. His fist came at me with such force I rolled across the coffee table into the wall where he proceeded to kick me. He walked away, took a shower, and went to bed. I slept on the floor again that night. That morning I woke to him having cyber-sex on the computer, and I thought, "I will be good, please not again," but instead he told me to get up: we were going to his parents' for lunch, we were bringing dessert. "Get up, get dressed, and make dessert. Don't you dare say anything to my family about this." I started bleeding in the shower, and I lost our baby that day. We went to his parents' house, and I happily talked about our life and future while not being able to lift my arms or turn my head and with blood in my panties. To this day, I still have bad headaches.

Again, he was wonderful for a few weeks and super attentive. He drove me to and from work, took me to my doctor's appointments, and sat in the room with me while the doctor did the exam. The attentiveness stopped one night when he had to "work late" again. I got a call from a "by the hour" motel: "Hello Miss, we have someone here who has checked in to our motel using your credit card and we'd like to verify permission." I raced over to the motel, and his car was in the parking lot, the fourth car I bought him in the year. I ran upstairs and started banging on the door, screaming at him. I had all the strength and rage at this point to confront him. He answered the door without his pants and this time I hit him. He ran after me, putting on his pants while running. I drove as fast as I could to the police department. He chased me. I ran into the police department and got attention as well as an emergency restraining order, good for 24 hours. A police officer made sure I got home safely, checked the apartment and advised that I barricade the door. He said that the police would do drive-bys through the night. In the morning I just had to go down to the court and I would be granted a two-week restraining order. I pushed my dad's leather recliner against the door, sank down to the ground, and cried until I fell asleep. Around 2 a.m. he pushed through the door. The police had been doing their rounds; my neighbor called and he was removed. This was it. Our relationship was done. I was done. This was my time to find that same strength that hit him to take care of me. It was my time. I moved out of the apartment into my car and lived in it until it was repossessed. At that time, I came through the revolving door to live on Mom's couch and rebuild my life.

The years went by and I continued to connect with emotionally unavailable and mean men because although I had rebuilt from nothing, I still didn't feel deserving. Eventually I met bum #2. He was only able to commit when he sensed I was moving away from him. I found myself pregnant again and was prepared to raise the baby on my own. At this point I owned a townhouse and was financially independent. Sadly, and randomly, I lost the baby.

I continued my pattern of picking the men that hit and kicked as a sign of love, the men that lied and cheated as a sign of stupidity, and the men that wanted me physically but would tell me I "just wasn't" the right one for their commitment, but I was perfect for a 10 p.m. "get together." With every one of the bums my self-esteem dropped, which would lead me to be vulnerable for the next. My self-esteem, my self-worth, was controlled by the people in my life, not just the men.

On a humid night in June, I had a dream. In my dream, Andy walked into my house in his full uniform. He looked at me and said, "Fishing Tackle, you know better. Get the BUMS out of your life. No giving up, no giving in. Do better, want better! You're better than all these idiots. No BUMS allowed." In my dream he then turned around, flashed me a smile, and walked out the door. I woke up covered in sweat; that was all too real. That morning as I was getting ready for work and listening to the news (for the weather report) I heard that he was killed in the line of duty.

History: *Andy joined the army in 1990. I was so afraid that I would never see him again, and because of that we never spoke again. Looking back, I made it all about me and my needs when I should have been celebrating Andy for his bravery, commitment, and family. Andy wasn't just my hero; he was a hero to all. Perhaps he was the real Superman.*

Andy died on June 13, 2003. As an army staff Sargent, Andy, then 30 years old, was stationed in Al Asad, Iraq for his second tour. The first was in Somalia. Andy was assigned to the 3rd Air Defense Artillery, 3rd Armor Calvary and, according to armchairgeneral.com's fallen heroes list, he "was returning from patrol on June 13th, 2003, when his armored personnel carrier went over a four-foot drop on the side of the road and rolled over....Andy helped one of his soldiers get out of the way but was struck by the vehicle himself and killed."

CHAPTER 3

SOUTHERN MAMAS AND SOUTHERN LOVE

In my heart, I knew what Andy said, in my dream, was true. No bums allowed! I put so much belief in the things people said to me and their opinions, etc. that I lost sight of me. I needed a fresh start, and that fresh start had to happen immediately. It was like ripping the band-aid off! It might sting, but as I say, "suck it up buttercup."

I listed my town house for sale that November and prepared to take a short sale. I wasn't sure where I would move, or even how I was going to move, but it was going to be out of state. I was going to do this, no excuses!

My first job offer came from a company in Honolulu; palm trees, sand in my toes, gorgeous sunsets, and an average temperature of 75 degrees, sign me up! Although this position would pay significantly less, the prospective employer assured me I would receive public assistance, and despite my misgivings I still wanted to make this move and change in my life. I found a 400 square foot loft, I made arrangements to ship my SUV, and then I learned that I would need to put my cat in confinement for up to nine months. Suddenly my gut was saying, "Um no!" I am not a crazy cat lady, by any means, and much prefer dogs, but I had been gifted the PERFECT cat and would not be separated. Position declined. I kept packing.

The next day I received a job offer in Goldsboro, North Carolina. All I knew about Goldsboro was that it was about 90 minutes from the Wilmington area. I accepted the job, rented an apartment online, and prepared to move. A few days later, I got a call that HR was requiring the position be filled by someone internal. I kept packing.

A day later, I received a call about a position in Raleigh, North Carolina. All I knew about Raleigh was that they had an airport. I accepted the position, and they wanted me to start in a week. I currently resided in Chicago and needed to get my house packed up, and start a new job in a city I knew nothing about, in ONE WEEK. I felt nothing other than anxiety. Holy smokes, this really was happening. I kept only what could fit in my SUV (and my cats, I had two now). Exactly three days after accepting the position, I left my vacant townhouse and headed east with a loaded SUV and two cats. Prior to leaving I rented an apartment online, I called a furniture store and ordered furniture by just telling the girl my style, and she arranged with the apartment complex to have the furniture delivered before I arrived so I'd have a bed to sleep in. I drove through the night in December 2004. I did it. I started fresh. Now to make the most of my fresh start.

Backstory: I had the perfect cat, Rocky! I was gifted Rocky after my second miscarriage. When my friend handed me Rocky, I asked her what I was supposed to do with this cat and she said, "Love it, be a mom," and that I did. About a year later I got a call that my friend found an abandoned car with a litter of newborn kittens. I adopted one. The vet estimated that she was maybe between three and five days old. I named her Gabriella Monkey and bottle fed her until she was old enough to eat on her own. Gabby was very timid and liked to hide in my box spring. Rocky would bring one pebble of food at a time to her and Gabby would stick her head out of the mattress and eat it.

My first day was interesting. I was sitting at a long conference table and minding my own business and I heard, "Ainet." My name is Annette, so I knew she couldn't have been talking to me. She proceeded and her voice got louder, and now she was banging on the table. "Ainet, Ainet, Ainet." A co-worker leaned over and said, "I think she's talking to you."

"Hello, are you speaking to me? My name is Annette," I said, to which she responded, "Yeah, you, Ainet. Are people really that rude in Chi-ca-go that they don't answer when called? Well, anyway, there's more than one way to lead the rat to the cheese."

The co-worker on the other side leaned in and said, "Don't mind her, she's from Johnston County, you know where they make the moonshine." These people became my family on the East Coast and my southern name became "Ainet."

After surviving my first ice storm, I adjusted to my new Southern name and wasn't getting lost as much, so I decided to start dating. I put my profile up on Match.com and came to realize that Raleigh had its share of bums too. I was lonely and I thought I needed a man to fill the void. Soon I realized I did not need a man and instead realized I WANTED a man in my life to share the wonders of life with me. Once I came to this realization I stopped responding until I had time to pray and go on a few adventures of my own. I came back, and I wrote a list of the qualities I wanted in a man and vowed to stick to that list. I made the list and put it in my bible, turning to God for his plan.

My List:
1. Over six feet tall (to reach the top shelf of the kitchen cabinets)
2. Good heart
3. Religious but not OVERLY religious
4. Handsome
5. Will be my best friend
6. Not previously married, no kids, no baggage
7. Will love me with all his heart
8. Will let me love him with all my heart
9. Kind hearted and gentle
10. Hair would be appreciated
11. Wants Children
12. Cleans the kitchen, takes out the trash, and helps with the laundry
13. Eats what I cook (Dear God, please help me learn to cook)

I was soon contacted on Match by a man that actually seemed "okay." I made sure to take it slow and so did he. We chatted for a month in email. I purchased one of those "get to know you" questions books, and every day I asked him a question. He answered and so did I. It was questions like toilet paper up or down, do you wash your feet in the shower, how often do you change your toothbrush, etc. Eventually he said to me, "Do you think we should meet?" I was hesitant. He was only 5'9, and he had an ex-wife and two children, but I did love our emails and I already felt like he could be my best friend. I closed the email and pretended I didn't see the question. I (um) was busy at work, sure that was it. After talking my Southern mama's ear off (the one that named me Ainet), I said yes and then freaked out (again). I was so worried it would be a 'one and done date' like all the others, would be a waste of my time, and then I would lose my email BFF. Southern mama's response: "If it is, we'll go have some moonshine and you'll forget about it after a swig or 10, or we can celebrate with some BBQ and moonshine when you get engaged, you choose." Our date was that following Friday, and although I had a closet full of clothes and shoes, I had absolutely NOTHING to wear. I ran to the mall and found the perfect cardigan and shoes.

I was so nervous that I had to do my makeup twice. I called to let Tom know I would be a few minutes late, and that was the first time I heard his voice. He had a very sweet southern sounding voice and I went into panic mode: "He's too nice, this is never going to work." I called up Southern mama and said, "I can't go. His voice is too sweet. Nice guys don't like me. Nope, I am good, I am gonna put on my jammies and call it a Friday night." Mama replied, "'The hell you say, it's 5:30 p.m. and you're younger than me. Go get your butt ready and I'll have the moonshine ready just in case." I had already learned not to go against Southern mama.

We met at the restaurant, and the first thing I noticed was his teeth, they were SO white and straight, the total opposite of mine. He was wearing a coral collared shirt (that his mama picked for the occasion), jeans, and white tennis shoes. The conversation was going well, and when he ordered his steak rare, I knew there was something there. We ended our date at the arcade and then talking (kissing) in his car. I left that parking lot feeling like God put me in North Carolina. This was God's plan. I had just had a wonderful date with a man only 5'9, previously married, with two kids, a vasectomy, and losing his hair. Tom was my destiny.

I met his kids, Jonathan (11, now 26) and Bailey (4, now 20), and we fell in love. We became a little family. Jonathan and Bailey approved of me and the family we became. This would be my happily ever after. I learned to love pig (true BBQ), and hush puppies, otherwise known to me as corn fritters. I learned that true sauce for BBQ should be vinegar based, not tomato based. Tomato based sauce is only for those in Western North Carolina and we were in Eastern North Carolina. I learned the proper way to refer to someone, "y'all," and if there was more than one it was "all y'alls." I learned to speak Southern and was better able to communicate with my Southern mama and boyfriend's family.

On New Year's Eve 2005 I had Tom, Jonathan, Bailey, my mom, and my stepfather over in my small apartment. We played cards, we laughed, the kids fell asleep, and Tom stayed over on the couch. The next morning, New Year's Day 2006, I woke him up, figuring he'd want to be awake before the kids, and he just stared at me and said, "I am going to spend the rest of my life loving you and proving my love for you every day." We were inseparable and madly in love. This was God's plan. On Valentine's Day he asked me to

move in with him; he had purchased a home the day before our first date. Of course, I said yes. So, we decided to go back to his house and start figuring out how to make it OUR house. On the way I got my first speeding ticket.

I really felt like he was going to propose. We had looked at a few rings but nothing was happening. Did I make a mistake moving in with him? Did I give him the milk for free? We decided to go away for the weekend to Highlands, North Carolina (way up in the mountains) and I thought to myself, if it doesn't happen this weekend I am going to move out. I hadn't broken the lease on my apartment yet, just in case. On Friday, March 31st we set out on our first vacation together. Tom said he wouldn't propose until he felt the timing was right, and I took that to mean he was having doubts. At each stop, I was hopeful he would "feel it." At our romantic dinner on Friday, at our stop at a romantic waterfall, sitting around the campfire, sitting on the deck of our treehouse. My heart sank as we went to sleep that night. I had accepted that he just wasn't going to propose. I awoke Saturday morning feeling optimistic again since he ordered a beautiful picnic basket for our hike. We sat in a field of sun flowers enjoying our picnic, I made sure to sit where the light would bounce off my eyes, let down my hair, and figured "what could be more right then this spot? This is it...it's going to happen." We finished our picnic and left without a proposal. Later that day Tom and I went gem mining, which was a new experience for me. I got my bucket of dirt, sat down at a table of muddy water, and began to shift through the rocks. Tom found this big rock, which looked like a clump of dirt, and got down on one knee and asked me to marry him...This, this is his big romantic moment? He says, "This is the moment. I love you. I will love you for the rest of my life. Will you marry me?" Both of us covered in dirt, Tom holding a rock, on April Fool's Day, and this is where he "feels it." My immediate response was "No, this is the meanest thing you could do." He persisted on his knee, telling me all the things he loved about me, reminding me that he was on his knee in dirt and I was leaving him hanging. He asked me again with people standing there and staring at us. This time, I said YES! He knew all along that the "clump of dirt" was a ruby, which he had made into my engagement ring. We were married March 24, 2007 in Chapel Hill, NC. Years later, I came to learn that he hated my first date cardigan.

I was learning to cook and feeding the family. I made chicken surprise all the time, and the surprise was if I burned it or not, if the kitchen was still in one piece, or if we were ordering take out. I later came to learn that my husband, Tom, and his two kids didn't really like my chicken surprise, or my taco salad, the two things I knew how to make the best, but they ate at least one serving and gave the rest to the dog. I even made roast for his cousin's family and they all stopped for fast food on the way home, which didn't make sense since I had a ton of leftovers (now it makes total sense).

I had often wondered why the dog was gaining so much weight, Tom was losing it, and the kids came over with food of their own. God answered my cooking prayers. I am a much better cook today. Actually, I am a pretty awesome cook, and everyone knows the messier the kitchen, the better the food tastes. Fortunately for me, I married a man who likes to clean the kitchen (list item #12).

Even after picking up and moving across country on my own in a week, I didn't realize my strength and my worthiness. In my mind, I was still that "fat, ugly" person, not worthy of love, not worthy of someone who would love me as much as I loved them. Not worthy of good people/things in my life. Moving like I did was incredibly brave, and I wasn't able to say that for quite some time. However, moving like I did showed me the power of me and opened my heart to wanting someone to share this with but being totally okay on my own. Once I got out of my head, out of my own way, and let my heart feel, once I believed in ME, once I gave up control and let God take the lead, wonderful things happened.

29

I found my strength in the dark when I stopped comparing myself to others and I started believing in the power of the life I deserved and not the life or thing I thought I needed. It happened when I believed in my "why" more than I believed in my "why not now." Finding strength in the dark happened when I found my own way to reach the top shelf in the kitchen.

"You'll be amazed at what you attract after you start believing in what you deserve."
~ Olivia Jade

CHAPTER 4

BABY FEVER, A LIGHT SWITCH, AND A FROGGY BEAR

Early on in our relationship, Tom and I talked about having children, and at that point he wasn't interested in having any more. We had just been dating a few months, so I didn't push but was hopeful. I had been learning to accept that I would not have children of my own but would love being a stepmother; although my heart longed to have an US baby, I knew Tom was my soul mate and I would be happy with our little family unit. Tom, always full of surprises, told me the night of the proposal that he also wanted us to have a baby and would have his vasectomy reversed after our honeymoon. We went to the same urologist that did his vasectomy and at our consult, when the doctor asked us how many children we wanted to have, Tom and I both responded at the same time. He said, "One, maybe two," and I said, "As many as we can." The doctor responded, "I'll just install a light switch, Tom!"

Once Tom heard about what would be involved in the surgery, I was sure he would say no, but instead he said, "It will be worth it, let's move forward," and we did! Tom was in surgery for three hours, came out, puked all over me and the nurses, and then went home with a bag of frozen peas since they work better than an ice pack.

The urologist suggested that we "get busy" within two to three weeks post-surgery, and that we did; however, our early attempts to conceive on our own were complicated and filled with tears. We tried boxers instead of briefs, we monitored my temperature and cervical fluid and even tried acupuncture, Chinese herbs, clomid (prescribed by my OB/GYN), keeping my feet elevated for an hour after sex, ovulation kits (with Tom coming home for a quickie on his break), essentially every "tried and true" option available, and yes, I even tried barking at the moon while jumping on one foot and eating a banana before standing on my head. Our month would go something like this: Day one of my cycle was heartbreaking, by day five we would start to feel optimistic, day seven I was reading the charts, day 17 I was looking at implantation calculators, day 21 I was searching for every possible symptom, day 24 I would be so positive that we were successful, and then on day 28, well...you know what happens. Rinse, recycle, repeat.

We weren't getting pregnant. It didn't seem fair as I wasn't even trying with my first two pregnancies. My OB/GYN suggested we see a reproductive endocrinologist.

Early testing with the reproductive endocrinologist showed that we had both male and female factor infertility but that we should begin with conservative interventions. The doctor helped us through two rounds of a medicated cycle IUI's (intrauterine insemination) and we were unable to conceive. Our doctor suggested we move on to IVF, but it would be very invasive.

> **Disclaimer:** I am not a medical professional, so I am going to speak about my experience and not the technical aspects to IVF (in vitro fertilization).

We had to sit through classes on the medicines (there were a lot), we had to sit through classes on how to do shots (there were a lot), and we had to go through a number of tests prior to starting the cycle. After all the classes, meds in hand and payment made, we were cleared to start. Before we knew it, it was time for the egg retrieval. Our doctor retrieved 10 eggs, of which only four were viable and only two seemed to be contenders after completing the ICSI (intracytoplasmic sperm injection) process, with one looking better than the other. The doctor, doing the fresh cycle transfer, gave us about a 1% chance of conception but encouraged us to think optimistically and start picking out names. Tom took me home where I did nothing but sit and incubate for five days and then wait another six days for my blood pregnancy test.

Friday, September 30th 2009, blood draw at 7:30 a.m.:
The doctor called me at 10 a.m. and said, "Congratulations, you are pregnant," and I replied, "Oh, since we don't have any more embryos do we do a second round of IVF?" The doctor spoke a bit louder: "Annette, listen to me. YOU ARE PREGNANT." Wait, what??? Did she just tell me I was pregnant? I needed to clarify. "I am not sure I understand, can you say that again?" to which the doctor spoke slower and repeated herself: "Annette, YOU ARE PREGNANT! Your hCG is really good. We'll repeat on Monday to make sure your numbers continue to rise." I was in denial, maybe I didn't hear her right, but she kept repeating herself. Did she really say I was pregnant? I called Tom at work. "Come home, right now... it's an emergency," and Tom came rushing home. I heard his tires squealing and a hard brake as he pulled into the driveway, and he ran into the house all scared. "What's going on? Is everything okay?"

33

"I don't know if everything is okay. That's why I called you home," I said.

"What's going on. Honey? Talk to me. Now your making me scared," he said.

I opened my mouth, not sure if I could get the words out. "Well, the doctor called and she kept telling me I am pregnant but we need to retest on Monday, so I am not sure if I am pregnant or if we need to try again but she said my numbers are really good and kept insisting I am pregnant" —deep breath— "but I just don't know what she meant by all this and I am really upset and not sure what to think—" Deep breath. As I continued, he interrupted.

"Honey, we are pregnant!" he said.

"How do you know?" I responded.

"Because the doctor wouldn't have said the words 'YOU ARE PREGNANT' if you weren't."

Oh, I guess he had a point.

"So, we are pregnant?" Squealing. "Why didn't she just say that? We're pregnant!"

Even after three positive pregnancy tests with good numbers, I couldn't believe I was pregnant and feared for the worst to happen. Anytime that I felt even the slightest bit of wetness between my legs, I ran to check for bleeding. My fears became a reality on October 11, 2009, I was five weeks pregnant and started bleeding. I called the doctor and she had me come in for an ultrasound.

When we got there, she ensured I understood that this early on in the pregnancy she might not be able to see anything, but let's hope to see a gestational sac. She continued with the ultrasound, and we did see a gestational sac and a fetal pole. This was much more than she thought we would see and felt everything looked good, so we repeated an hCG test to make sure my numbers weren't dropping, and the numbers were continuing to rise. We left comforted and happy to see what looked like a fish, and I was the fishbowl. The bleeding slowed down but never really stopped.

A few days later the bleeding got worse. The doctor couldn't see me, so we went to our general practitioner (who was also an OB). He did an exam and said that the bleeding was not a good sign but that my cervix was closed and it didn't seem like an immediate concern for miscarriage. He sent me home on bed rest. In the middle of the night the bleeding got worse and I was changing pads once an hour. Tom decided we should go to the ER, who did not consider me a priority because I was so early in my pregnancy. I was finally seen around 3 a.m. The ultrasound was good and the numbers were rising, but the ER doctor felt I should terminate the pregnancy because of the bleeding. His reasoning was that first trimester bleeding indicates a non-viable pregnancy. I refused! Tom supported my right to refuse! The ER doctor actually had the nerve to call in a psychiatrist to have me evaluated for a psychiatric hold because of my refusal. The psychiatrist agreed with me as well, and I was sent home on bed rest. At six weeks, while I was still bleeding, we saw fish's beautiful heartbeat, and at seven weeks we heard that sweet sound.

At eight weeks I graduated from weekly visits with the reproductive endocrinologist and was officially being seen by the OB clinic. However, the bleeding continued, and I was in the OB's office at least once a week for ultrasounds. The doctor always reassured me that the baby was healthy but had no idea why the bleeding continued. This all was taking quite a toll on the both of us emotionally, and I was having serious anxiety. There was absolutely nothing I could do to keep our baby safe, and while I knew lying in bed wasn't the answer, I felt that I was at least doing something for my baby. I cried every day, all day, which

I am sure was just hormones (I said, sarcastically). Tom kept saying to me, "We have to keep the faith. We have to pray," and that I did.

Even through the prayers and the support, I was terrified and, quite honestly, sad. I "ugly" cried daily, and on a good day I may have only cried once. Tom came to bed one night and looked at me. I didn't smile back. He then leapt into bed like a frog. Something I had never seen before. Who was this frog I married? His nickname was already "Tommy Bear," and after 2.5 years of marriage I learned he was a frog. I had actually married a frog! I don't think I have ever laughed so hard, and I just kept saying through the laughter, "You're a frog, my husband's a frog." Tommy became known as my froggy bear (a bear with frog legs), and our baby became a tadcub (half tadpole, half bear). Check out his tattoo!

I was 10 weeks on the day of the biggest soccer game of the year (my husband coached and my stepdaughter Bailey, now nine, played) and also Bailey's birthday party, and I had the worst cramps. So bad that my mother-in-law, Patti, stayed with me while Tom was at the game. I was doubled over in pain, crying. I had never felt so much pain. Patti, a nurse, gave me some coca cola and a tums just to see if that helped, and to my embarrassment, it did! I let out the loudest, most unladylike burp, and I felt better. Whew, time to get ready to party.

The party was starting at 7 p.m. I started to have some cramps again around 6:15 p.m. and took another tums, I figured it was just annoying gas, but while I did have another loud burp, at 6:30 p.m. blood started to drip through my panties. I went to the bathroom and passed what looked like a large blood clot. Patti got the party started while Tom and I called the doctor. The OB on call, who was already familiar with me, said that it sounded like I miscarried and we should come into the office the next day, Sunday, at 9 a.m., so she could do an ultrasound to confirm and a D&C the same day. The doctor asked Tom to take the clot out of the toilet, put it in a bag, and put the bag in the freezer so we could bring it to the appointment if needed. Tom did, as asked, while crying and shaking. The cramping was gone, and all of the sudden I felt better physically and destroyed emotionally, but we had 25 kids and their parents over, so we put on our happy hosting faces and celebrated our nine-year-old's birthday. Outside of the three of us (me, Tom, and Patti), nobody had a clue about our broken hearts, and the birthday party was amazing!

With broken hearts and a frozen baggie, we were off to the doctor's. We started with the ultrasound while the doctor had the nurse reserve the OR. The doctor apologized and understood how hard this was on us and turned the screen away so we couldn't see.

Something didn't seem right, I thought, because the doctor put her hand over her heart and didn't speak. In my head I was pleading with the doctor to get this over with, and in my heart I was begging God to let our little tadcub be okay. The doctor turned on the large screen so we could see our tadcub was fine, swimming and dancing around her swamp, and the heartbeat was really strong. The doctor moved the wand away from tadcub and said, "This is what's causing your bleeding! You have a sub-chronic hemorrhage, which will most likely resolve itself." She explained, "It's fairly common in the first trimester."

She ended our appointment by saying, "Annette, you have to find some way to enjoy this pregnancy." I thought to myself, "Um hello, nothing has been enjoyable since October 11th. Every day I have lived in fear, being told I will likely lose this baby." I just responded, "Doctor. I don't know how. It's been a lot," and to that she took out her prescription pad and prescribed nightly foot rubs for a minimum of 10 minutes per foot with unlimited refills and handed the prescription to Tom as she said, "Here, fill this." The bleeding continued after this for a few more weeks, but we were less nervous. At 12w1d the bleeding stopped and I didn't bleed for the remainder of the pregnancy.

The doctor was right; the foot rubs really did help, and we were enjoying every minute of the pregnancy, and Froggy Bear reminded me that it was because we held onto faith and we trusted in God. Feeling tadcub move at 14 weeks was the most amazing experience, and at 20 weeks we had our anatomy scan. Tadcub was a very happy healthy baby girl! Jonathan and Bailey were with us at the ultrasound and were thrilled! Froggy Bear and I looked at each other and said at the same time, "We need to name her Faith," and we prepared our lives for a baby girl.

Following the ultrasound, we went straight to the baby store and started Faith's wardrobe. We also looked at strollers. The stroller sales associate asked us about our stroller budget, and I replied, "About $150." She was shocked and exclaimed, "For your PRIMARY stroller?" and proceeded to show us a $1200 stroller that could be used to carry golf clubs when the baby aged out of the stroller. Tom started to panic and said, "Honey, what's your plan. Don't you have a spreadsheet or a project plan or something?" to which I responded, "I guess you shouldn't have thrown out my binder for Disney World, huh!" Tom gave me a stare and said, "Project manager, GO!"

At 27 weeks I was diagnosed as a gestational diabetic and put on diabetes medicine, and at my 33-week diabetic scan, Faith didn't move as they hoped, so I was sent for some sort of fancy scan at the high-risk OB clinic that same day. The perinatologist was concerned about Faith's heart and a possible malfunction and sent us to see a neonatal cardiologist for an evaluation.

If we didn't know it by now, we had our confirmation: Faith would be strong willed and march to the beat of her own drummer. The neonatal cardiologist pulled out all the tricks to get Faith into the right position to examine her heart, and she was not cooperating. He even turned the table nearly upside down. The only answer, since we couldn't get an answer, was to transfer my care for the duration of the pregnancy to the high-risk clinic. I would be seen three times a week and induced at 39 weeks. The doctor was concerned that while I would carry to term, Faith might not survive childbirth. We prayed but also carried on with the pregnancy, holding on to faith.

Jonathan begged and pleaded with me not to have the baby until after his 16th birthday on May 19th. I was doing my best and keeping my legs crossed as much as possible. Of course, at 10 p.m. on May 18th I started having labor pains every two minutes. I called the OB on call and they said to come on in and get checked out. Suitcase in hand, we drove to the hospital in silence. Tom was preparing to be a nervous new dad, and I was nervous about telling Jonathan we had the baby ON his birthday. The OB said I was about 1-2cm dilated and sent me home. Whewww, that was a close one.

At our second-to-last high-risk clinic visit, Faith was not moving much. The nurse gave me some orange juice and that helped. As the doctor proceeded with the ultrasound, she was poking my belly. When we finally got to see Faith on the ultrasound, she was a happy tadcub and gave the doctor the middle finger with a scrunched-up face. My guess is that she was taking her morning nap and we woke her up.

We induced labor at 39 weeks, and of course Faith had to be born on her terms. After 20 hours in labor, the doctors broke my water and she was born within an hour. Right between the night and day shifts with the night charge nurse and the day charge nurse bickering over how dilated I was or wasn't. Faith Nellie Beatrice Pearson was born after 30 minutes of pushing on 6/6/2010 at 7:32 a.m. weighing 7lbs 6oz, and we never got a height because the nurses forgot to measure her. As soon as she was delivered, the NICU doctor whisked Faith away before I could hold her. As the doctor was reaching for his stethoscope, Faith rolled over on the table. The doctor gave her an Apgar score of 9 out of 10 and handed her back to me. I held her, kissed her, and nursed her, and then Faith went for an echo with her daddy while the nurses cleaned me up and brought me to my post-labor room. Faith's final heart diagnosis was A BAD ULTRASOUND! She was 100% healthy.

Backstory: Faith's middle names come from her great grandmothers, Nellie Anderson and Beatrice Friedman. Two of the strongest women Tom and I know. Nellie lived to be 106 years old, still beating us all at cards right up until the end. Beatrice lived to be 92 and could tell you anything about Lucy and Ricky Ricardo and her latest romance novel until the end.

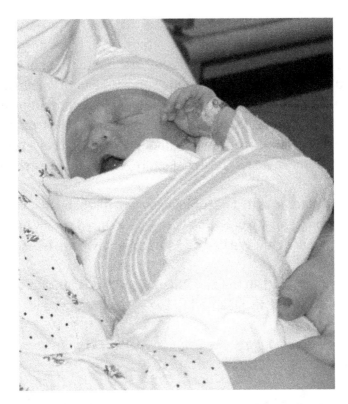

The discharging OB gave me an official diagnosis of anxiety on the discharge papers and on Faith's birth records. I was angry; I felt I had every reason to be anxious, but the doctor did not agree. I carried this anger with me for quite some time until I realized that the anger over something I knew to be true was contributing to my post-partum depression and I needed to let it go. The truth is that I did have anxiety during my pregnancy, and I still have anxiety to this day. Nothing, no diagnosis or lecture, would change my reality.

I was going home with a beautiful baby girl, this baby that I dreamt of for so long, and the baby that I prayed for since I got my mansion. We found our Faith. We had our miracle and we are blessed.

I found my strength in the dark when I found my faith and gave my fears to God. And also learned to live with a froggy bear.

"Start where you are. Use what you have. Do what you can."
~ Arthur Ashe

CHAPTER 5

MAYBE BABY, TAKE 2!

On our final day in the hospital, Tom and I sat looking at our perfect baby, and we were completely in love with her and also with each other. We also were in agreement, she was going to be a handful and she was going to keep the both of us on our toes, which she still does at 10.

Life with a newborn was amazing. I loved all the little sounds, the big cries, the little cries, the poopy diapers, the really poopy diapers, middle of the night feedings, tummy time, and doing the mommy rock, you know, standing in one spot, rocking side to side. We did have a bit of trouble with nursing; the nurse in the hospital said my boobs were too overwhelming and scared the baby. This of course freaked me out and I was completely worried that I was going to smother Faith while nursing.

I received a call offering me a permanent position while in labor. Of course, I accepted but then also told the HR rep I would need to call her back as the doctor was walking in saying, "Let's check your cervix." However, until the new job started, I had to go back to work at three weeks since I was an independent contractor and had to keep the customers happy. Fortunately, I worked from home. Jonathan and Tom's cousin mostly stayed with Faith upstairs while I worked downstairs. Hearing my three-week-old crying while I was on a conference call and couldn't do anything to help broke my heart, but the reality was the baby needed diapers and it took both Tom and me to financially keep the house going. We were, after all, a family of five.

Side Story: I got caught pumping while on a work call! I needed to pump; my supply was in demand, so I made sure every two hours to have the baby or the pump (if not both) on the boob. It was time and I was stuck presenting on a call. I figured if I put the machine under the desk and covered myself and the machine that the sound would be muffled enough and nobody would notice. It wasn't like I would be complimenting myself for pooping on the call, which actually happened but it wasn't me pooping. I was the one yelling, "Mute, mute, mute, someone isn't on mute." Anyway, I just got flowing into the pump and someone said, "Does someone have a machine on? It sounds like a pump. Whoever it is, please go on mute?" I was facilitating the call, so sorry, but I can't go on mute. Deal with it. When we need to feed or pump, we have the right and should have every ability to do so.

The family participated in the nightly "boobie booty dance parade," which was the key to everyone in the house getting four to five hours of sleep. Faith had a very loud cry when she was hungry. At 9 p.m. we'd play AC/DC's "Thunderstruck," Tom would pick Faith up, and the five of us would parade around the house singing and dancing so that Faith would be wide awake and ready to eat. We repeated this performance nightly, no ticket necessary to see the show.

As scary as the pregnancy was with Faith, I loved being pregnant (the good parts of our pregnancy). I loved feeling her hiccup and the kicks. I loved it all. I love being a mommy, and I knew as soon as I heard Faith's first cry that I was always meant to be Faith's mommy!

After Faith was born, Tom told me we could have as many children as possible as long as we had them before his 40th birthday. He wanted to have a large family but didn't want the kids to push his wheelchair. The doctor told us at discharge that our best chance of getting pregnant naturally was now and said we could resume intercourse in four to six weeks. We took this very seriously, and at six weeks we started with temperatures, timed intercourse, ovulation tests, etc. We realized if we were successful that we'd have two babies under the age of one but that was a chance we were willing to take. At my six-week post-partum visit, I told the doctor our plan, and she was completely shocked and immediately went to go check my post-partum depression test results. No, Doc, I can assure you that I have not lost my mind.

Needless to say, we weren't successful but were quite persistent. While I was treasuring every moment with Faith, every diaper blowout, every 2 a.m. feeding, every hug, kiss, "coo," etc., I couldn't help but feel a bit sad that this would be my last time feeding a two-week-old, that this would be my last time rocking a nine-month-old to sleep. I had accepted that we weren't going to conceive naturally and also that IVF was no longer a financial option for us, and I was jealous of Tom for getting to do this three times. Why can't having a baby be as easy for me as it was for Barbie? I mean, all she had to do was buy a baby for $1.50, open the box, and throw the glitter.

By the time Faith was one, Tom and I were running the community soccer league and he was coaching. Things were quite busy at the Pearson house. In addition to Bailey playing soccer, she was also in gymnastics and on the weekends, we felt like our mini-van went this way and that way, all the weekend long.

Faith was quite the little mommy, just like I was, and she started to take care of her baby dolls. At two she would say, "Me want bebe." She was also quite determined to be a dancer like her cousins. At three, Faith was continually asking for a baby brother. We longed for another child too, and upon learning that I now had IVF benefits at work, we started IVF round number two with the same doctor that gave us our Faith.

This round of IVF was much more difficult because we had a toddler and I was working full-time. I had not been working during our IVF cycle with Faith. The doctors had trouble getting me to the optimal levels, which they said was likely due to stress and not enough rest. We persisted, and I rested as often as possible and again before we knew it, we were at egg retrieval day. Oh, the excitement and nerves. We went in feeling confident that we would have a positive outcome given how our cycle went with Faith. I am pretty sure we were strutting like peacocks. The doctor retrieved four eggs, of which three were mature, and one became an embryo after being fertilized by ICSI, and this one would be transferred at our day three fresh transfer. Again, I sat and was an incubator for five days, and then we waited until 11 days after the transfer for the pregnancy test. Around day eight, my boobs were hurting (I write a lot about my boobs, don't I?) and I was nauseated and extremely hormonal. In my heart I knew this meant pregnancy, and I was hopeful that this pregnancy would be amazing, the perfect pregnancy that you read about in books. On cycle day nine, I started to bleed and the bleeding became that of a full period. I called the nurse, and she said that this didn't mean good things for a positive outcome, but she still wanted me to come in on day 11 and be tested, so I did. The doctor called at 10:30 a.m. and the call went something like this:

"Hello," I said.

The doctor replied, "Hi Annette, it's Dr. XXX."

"I know, its negative," I said.

The doctor replied, "Actually no, it's not. Your hCG is 35, so you're pregnant. It's just not as high as it should be. There is either a problem with the pregnancy or late conception or both. Come in for another blood draw in 72 hours. If the numbers double, I am less concerned."

I honestly didn't know what to feel. I refused to let myself feel happy because I was so scared, but I also realized that I had to be as positive as possible for myself, the baby, Faith, Tom, Jonathan, and Bailey. Of course, only Tom knew what was going on. I also had a paper due for my master's program about "how to solve the world's health crisis," which was a mouthful and a 40-page paper due Sunday that I was JUST starting on Friday. We also had Bailey with us that weekend and we didn't want her to know. We just wanted the family to enjoy being together and for us to have quality family time. Tom and I would go into our bedroom for the daily progesterone shot (in my butt). After the shot, Tom and I would both cry and hold each other then compose ourselves, wash our tears away, and leave our bedroom being the happiest parents, ready to play a round of hide-and-seek. That Sunday morning, I went in for the blood draw and kept my head down, writing my paper, trying my hardest not to think about it. But in the afternoon the call came and the doctor said, "I am so sorry, Annette, your hCG level is only 38. This is not a viable pregnancy. Please stop taking your meds so that your body can release the embryo and you'll get your period." We were devastated, but we both knew we had to keep our feelings behind closed doors so nobody would know.

In our hearts we felt that this baby would also be a girl and we would name her Emme Sophia. We know our Emme is in heaven and we will see her again someday.

BTW, I got an A+ on the paper.

I felt hopeless. This IVF attempt was the last of our savings and insurance benefits. I felt alone, and I questioned God's presence and intent with my life. I didn't feel like I could discuss my feelings because, to me, it seemed like Tom just went on with life and there was an expectation that I would too, but I didn't know how. My sadness continued behind closed doors, but I never stopped taking care of the family, I still was going strong in my master's program,

MAYBE BABY, TAKE 2!

work was thriving, and I was being promoted. I just cried alone, in the shower, while going to the bathroom. I would suddenly need to use the bathroom every time I heard Faith say, "Me want bebe," and it was on these bathroom trips that I wouldn't leave the door open so I could be Faith's jungle gym, and I would turn the water on so nobody could hear me cry. Each day the crying got less and less and I focused more and more on being the wife and mom that everyone deserves.

When she was three years old, I was approached by Faith's preschool teacher, who said, "Congratulations, I hear you are expecting?" "I am?" I replied, and the teacher said, "Faith says her mommy is having a baby." I assured her that I was not pregnant and we spoke with Faith. Faith said, "I know we are going to have a baby, Mommy. I pray every night for a baby and God won't let me down."

This conversation reminded me of two things: 1) God's plan for my life and 2) before all of this I was a woman, not just a baby factory, and I still was that woman who was stuck in the baby making assembly process. It was time to put away the granny panties and step into a little something lacy, and it was time to stop wearing maternity clothes because I was not pregnant, and it was time to take care of me. I remembered that while having a large family is in God's hands, I had (have) a wonderful husband, our (miracle) US baby, and two of the best stepchildren that I could ever ask for, and this was the perspective I needed. I found my strength in the dark when I listened to God's plan.

CHAPTER 6

CALIFORNIA, HERE WE COME!

Over a year later, things with work were busy and I had a new boss. Tom and I were still living in Durham, North Carolina, and I was working from home full-time with my new boss located in California. I was also a boss myself, now (fancy, right? Not really), and some of my team members were also in California. My boss had me traveling to California one week out of six to be in the office, requiring that I leave Sunday morning and return that following Saturday. I cried most of the way to California and felt like I was willing the plane to fly faster coming home. I cried every night. Faith was three and I thought, "How could she possibly understand Mommy being gone this long?"

Faith would send me off with one of her stuffed animals, and I would wear one of Tom's shirts to sleep. As supportive as Tom was, this was taking a toll on the family, on us as a couple, and I was feeling more and more like I was failing as a mommy and putting work ahead of my family's needs. I remember one particular trip where Tom and Faith dropped me off at the airport Sunday morning at 7 a.m. EST, flying from Raleigh to Atlanta to Oakland and finally into Burbank/Hollywood airport, arriving at 5 p.m. PST/8 p.m. EST. For the return I was picked up from my hotel at 4 a.m. PST/7 a.m. EST in the pouring rain, arriving at the airport before they opened at 5:30 a.m. (for a 6:30 a.m. flight) and sitting outside without an umbrella, boarding the plane in the rain, flying to Ohio to Atlanta and finally into Raleigh, and Tom picking me up from the airport at 5 p.m. EST. Faith and Tom would always be waiting for me by baggage claim, and Faith would run to me, saying, "Mommy, Mommy, Mommy, I love you Mommy, don't ever leave again," and Tom would be open arms, kissing me deeply saying, "I missed you so much, don't ever leave us again." We'd stop for dinner on the way home, and he would be snoring by 8:30 p.m.

That winter we had a terrible ice storm with a tree coming down blocking our way in or out of the neighborhood, and taking out our electricity too. Every day the sun would come out, melting the ice and snow, but by sunrise the next morning everything was frozen again. Since everything shuts down for an ice storm, Faith's preschool was closed for 11 days and we didn't go anywhere. Shortly after, my boss said, "I think it's time you move out to California. We'll pay for your moving expenses." I told him that I didn't think that was the best thing for our family since we'd be leaving Jonathan (19 and in college) and Bailey (13 and moving up into HS) in North Carolina with their mom and we'd be across the country in California. I was reminded that there was a need to be onsite, and if I couldn't fulfil it, they would have to replace me with someone local. At the same time, Tom's employer was talking about layoffs too. We both couldn't be out of work. We thought about it long and hard, weighed the pros and cons, figured out a plan to be present and intentional in Jonathan and Bailey's life, and made the decision to move to California. My gut hurt! How could I do this and take Tom and Faith away from their family, his children, her brother and sister, but knowing we'd have a plan to "make it work," we realized we needed to make the move.

The house was listed for sale, and the moving company would be coming to pack the boxes in three weeks. In the meantime, we spent as much time with the family as possible. Faith had her second dance recital. I also danced in that recital (jazz and tap), and we said goodbye to our dance family. Faith celebrated her fourth birthday with family and friends, and in a blink of an eye, the three weeks had passed. It literally happened that fast, or at least it felt like it.

After the movers packed over 500 boxes, the moving truck arrived. I'd estimate the truck to be around 40 feet, and we were sharing it with another family also moving from Durham to (somewhere in) California. The house was empty, and I felt empty too. I had so many doubts, so much guilt, and so much sadness for the family and friends we were leaving behind. The guilt was overwhelming and so was the anxiety. Tom and the kids were happy about the move; moving to California was huge. Bailey was excited for all the opportunities she would have during the summer and holidays. Jonathan was excited to spend school breaks without humidity and maybe meet some famous people. Faith was excited about the beaches and the opportunity to become a "real dancer on stage." I just couldn't get there. I couldn't be as excited as they were. I felt like I was breaking Tom's heart and making him choose between me and Faith and his kids and family. I just couldn't help but feel like I was a monster.

We planned to rent an apartment until we got settled and then would look for a house. We picked out a 983 square foot apartment on the "second floor," sight unseen. Mind you, we were leaving a 3,000 square foot home on half an acre to move to a 983 square foot, two-bedroom apartment. Since the house had not sold yet and we'd have both rent and a mortgage to pay, Tom would come back to North Carolina and stay until the house sold. He, along with Bailey, would drive us out to California then return to North Carolina, and when it was time, he would put his car on a truck and fly out with the two dogs. Tom and I were the inseparable couple, and the only time we were away from each other was when I traveled, and, well, we know how we both did with that. Not only was this move taking Tom away from his family, it would take him away from me and Faith too. This was just too much.

Our last night in the house, before we headed out west, I was pacing, crying, and I confessed to Tom that I couldn't do this. We needed to get our furniture back and NOT move. That was the first time that Tom gave me the stare down and said, "While you're losing your mind, I am going to get some milk for breakfast in the morning" and left for the grocery store. While he was gone, I prayed to God, "God, I just don't know what to do. Please give me some sort of sign of your plan," and I cried.

Faith and I are fiercely afraid of snakes, any kind of snake; we do not discriminate. Tom came home and took a few minutes to get in the house. I figured he was on the phone with his dad talking about how crazy I am. When he came in, he said, "Did you ask God for a sign while I was out?" "Yes, how did you know?" I replied. Tom picked up his phone, opened his pictures, and handed me his phone, and as he did, he said, "Here's your sign!" He handed me a picture of a three-foot long copper head snake that was about three inches thick that was coiled up in our driveway. Thank you, God, for the sign. This didn't change the guilt, but at least I knew God approved. I didn't sleep that night. I had to go outside in the morning, and what if the snake was outside waiting for me?

Tom planned to leave by 7 a.m. EST. This time he had his own binder as he wanted to make this into a vacation/adventure as we drove across the country, >3000 miles. I figured that after last night, this probably wasn't the best time to bring up my Disney World binder.

CALIFORNIA, HERE WE COME!

We pulled off the driveway at 9:30 a.m., first stopping for breakfast and then snacks for the road. We left Durham at 11 a.m. Our goal for that first night was Alabama, the next day El Campo, Texas to spend the Fourth of July with family. We spent day three driving through Texas into New Mexico. Day four we spent some time with a high school friend of mine in Albuquerque. Day five was at the Grand Canyon, and on day six we made the final descent into California, staying with a family friend until we could get in the apartment. On day seven, we got the keys to our new apartment.

I completely underestimated 983 square feet. I also didn't truly understand what the second floor meant for a building without elevators. The kitchen was such that if the refrigerator or dishwasher was open, then it was a kitchen for one. The majority of the living space was in the master bedroom, which we decided to give to Faith so she'd have a place for her toys since there was no room in the living room and so that guests could bunk with Faith. Tom and I took the small bedroom, Faith got her own bathroom, and we used the hall/guest bathroom. Before leaving NC, we had separated boxes for things that would go to the apartment and things that would go to storage. Tom and I quickly realized we'd need to send more to storage, and we ended up filling a 10x12 storage shed to the ceiling tall and to the door wide. The second floor was really three sets of stairs up, no joke. I lost a ton of weight while we lived in the apartment and my butt was truly amazing.

Tom and Bailey stayed for one additional week and we explored together, went to different churches, and did the most we could before they left. The week went by too fast, and before we knew it Saturday morning was upon us. We went out for breakfast and got back in time for the shuttle to pick them up. We didn't really get to say good-bye with the shuttle double parked and honking. Tom and Bailey walked out the door and Faith and I cried. Both of our hearts broke as we watched Tom and Bailey get in the shuttle. We were on our own in a place that should feel like home but

55

instead felt like a strange city. I was lost physically and emotionally. I wanted to take Faith for a walk or to the playground, but she just wanted to sit in "Daddy's spot" and watch a movie, and honestly, I was just fine with that too. Sunday morning, Faith and I went to church with a friend and we checked Faith into Sunday school and she immediately ran off to play. While sitting in worship, I couldn't remember if I actually turned the stove off or not after making Faith eggs and ran back to the apartment, up the three flights of stairs, only to find out that I did but my heart was too broken to remember.

Faith didn't need her own room because she slept with me. Better said, she slept and I cried. What did I just do? What did I do to our family? We were supposed to be together, not divided across the country. That next day, Monday, Faith started her new school and I started working full-time in the office. I couldn't cook in THAT kitchen, Faith only wanted to eat out, and I had no interest in eating. We just wanted to rush home after work and school to spend the evening with Daddy on the computer. We put the computer at the table while Faith ate, we put the computer on the couch while we watched TV, we brought the computer into the bedroom to tuck Faith in, and I would shut the computer down when Tom was in bed. Tom would call me at 4 a.m. PST/7 a.m. EST on his way to work, and most of the time I hadn't even been to sleep yet.

The first Friday Tom was gone, he didn't call me at 4 a.m. I figured he must have overslept, so I called Tom, but there was no answer. I proceeded to get myself up and ready, then Faith, and we tried to call him again. Still no answer. I was getting worried and called his work phone. No answer. Where was my husband! I had hoped the answer would be that he didn't answer because he was on a plane to surprise us. As I pulled into the work parking lot my phone rang.

"Hey honey!" He sounded groggy and not feeling well.

"Hey, did you oversleep? WE missed you this morning."

There was silence. "Honey, Dad just brought me home from the ER." My heart sank. Tom is very healthy and the only medical care he had received had been for his vasectomy, vasectomy reversal, colds, and when he had a stuck marshmallow at Christmas.

"What's wrong, are you okay?" I said in a panic.

"Honey, I had the worst pains in my stomach at 2 a.m. and had to call Dad to take me to the ER. Honey, it's my gallbladder and I need to have it out. I need to have surgery."

I was in tears. "Faith and I will be 'home' tomorrow to take care of you."

You could hear the relief in his voice as he said, "Thank you, Honey. I need you!"

I ran into the office, called my boss, told him what was happening, and booked two tickets to Durham. We were at the airport at 3 a.m. for a 5:00 a.m. flight out of LAX. Faith didn't know her daddy was sick; she just thought we were rushing back because we missed him so much. We ran to him and I cried so hard. We were together again. Tom said, "It's okay, Honey, you're here now, and we are together, everything is going to be okay, we are together." I didn't know if I could ever let him go again.

Tom borrowed a bed from his dad for Faith, and she slept in her old room that night (the nursery). We left Tom with some furniture since he was staying at the house until it sold, which he would sell before he left, so we were able to settle in as a family. It felt so good to be back in our home, sleeping next to my husband and watching my daughter sleep in her room. Faith's nursery was decorated like a garden. I had a sky painted on the ceiling with a lamp that looked like the sun, the rug on the floor resembled grass with flowers, and I had butterflies flying up her wall. I loved being in Faith's room, playing with her, rocking her to sleep; now four, she would still let me rock her. I slept for the first time in a week, wrapped in Tom's nook, my sleeping space.

Monday, we went to the doctor to schedule Tom's surgery. The doctor didn't think he'd be able to get him in for surgery for a month. We begged and explained that I flew in from California, and the doctor was kindly able to reschedule his calendar and get Tom in for Thursday at 8 a.m. In the meantime, we were able to spend time with Jonathan and Bailey. We were together as a family again. Faith went to her (former) preschool and loved seeing her friends. Patti went with us to the hospital and sat with me. That guilt I had been feeling intensified. It took Tom being sick to bring us all together again. It took being back in NC to sleep, and our family and friends were with us, no questions asked.

As it turns out, the gallbladder incident was likely triggered because Tom was eating cookie dough and queso with chips; he was lost without us too. Bailey told me about what he was eating and how sad he was. Tom never mentioned it. The surgery went well, and Faith and I were scheduled to fly back on Saturday. Tom insisted on driving us to the airport. That Friday we had a long talk about how the separation of just one week impacted us all and re-declared our intense love for each other. We also got an offer on the house that day with a 30-day escrow. That was it. We both knew right away that Tom would go back to work on Monday, give his two-week notice, and officially move to California. Tom brought Bailey, and they flew with our two dogs. We were together again on August 1st, 2014. We all had a great week together, and Tom and Bailey got to explore and have quality time before Bailey returned home to start her freshman year in high school. She was excited to return at Christmas for two weeks.

Both of our mothers came to see us and enjoyed California. Tom's mom came for Labor Day and my mom for Thanksgiving. Bailey was with us for Christmas, and Jonathan came too. We were all together for Christmas, sitting around our dining room table, and the next day we were off to Disneyland.

After getting terrible food poisoning from grocery store sushi, Tom and I bought a house and happily left our tiny apartment. We made sure to buy a house big enough to have rooms for Bailey and Faith, a guest room, and a nursery. We hadn't given up hope.

When we were living in North Carolina, I felt an intense amount of pressure to build "the perfect home," to bring the family together, to keep everyone happy, and to be the perfect wife. We would host Thanksgiving and Christmas and so many of the holidays, we would bring everyone together for an occasional Sunday dinner, and I would always plan out the perfect menu. I spent $1000 on groceries one year for Thanksgiving, the year we had 40 people over. While I loved having everyone over, and it was my choice to do so, I felt like I needed to do it. I needed to do it to prove that I was a good wife, to prove I could cook (now), to prove to myself that I was capable, to make magical holiday memories for the kids, and to prove I was worthy. The truth is, I didn't feel worthy. I didn't feel like I was a good enough wife, mom, stepmom, daughter-in-law, sister-in-law, etc. So, I hosted a lot. It was a ton of work, and when everyone left, I judged everything I did, everything I made, everything I said and felt like it was all wrong. I love entertaining, but did I really need to make 15 cornish game hens? Was the homemade eggnog, fresh pies, and two turkeys really necessary? I was never going to be a cooking, baking wonder woman anyway, and my meringue never seemed to meringue.

When we moved to California, it was just the three of us, maybe five if we had out-of-town visitors. It took a long time to learn how to cook a family meal for three, and we still seem to have a lot of leftovers. Just the other night I made beef spare ribs in the crockpot and Faith didn't like them. I was okay with that. I didn't rush off to make her something else. I am not perfect, my home is a mess (go ahead and check for dust, you'll find it), the laundry is backed up, and my go-to style is a messy bun. Oh well! This is me! I'd rather chill with the family or have a date with my husband than hand out coasters.

I found my strength in the dark when I moved my family across country and Tom and I worked together to build a new life! I found my strength when I stopped worrying about the right number of side dishes and realized that I don't need to prove myself; I am me, and when it comes to knowing me, you get what you get and you get upset or you don't, the choice is yours. I will not stress over *your* opinions. Oh, and the holidays are more magical when things are simple, like when I am at the table and not in the kitchen, and yet I still manage to have "glitter" all over the house, except now I enjoy the glitter vs. stress to clean it up.

I knew I had found my strength in the dark when I ran a 5K with my friends, dressed like a Valley Girl, in 2015. About a quarter of a mile after the start line, I tripped over a hole in the ground. I didn't give up and finished the 3.10686 miles, running on the outside of my foot while my friends finished way ahead of me. I sprinted across the finish line (for the first time in my life), on a broken foot. My friends were right there at the finish line with wine and celebration. I found my strength in the dark when I didn't give up or give in even with a broken foot.

CHAPTER 7

MAYBE BABY, TAKE 3!

Tom's new job in California provided us with insurance benefits for a third IVF cycle in 2016. With the help of the doctor and the lab, we produced two viable embryos. As a result of our previous attempts, the doctor suggested that we perform PGS testing. PGS testing is genetic testing done on embryos resulting from an IVF procedure so that the embryos that are the most likely to result in a pregnancy are identified based on embryo grading, as explained by igenomics.com. We were not concerned about gender; we just knew that we needed a positive outcome and not another loss. The embryologist would select the best embryo for each transfer based on the likelihood of implantation, which was determined by the embryo score/report card.

Tom flew out to North Carolina on Thursday, August 4th for Jonathan's wedding. Faith had auditions for her dance company and the doctor did not want me flying because of my previous bleeding after embryo transfers. I was really sad to miss my stepson's wedding, and I hope that one day they will renew their vows so that I can be there, which I know is a bit selfish on my part. Being a former event planner, I did plan their rehearsal dinner and the luncheon between the ceremony and the reception. I sent Tom on his way with everything paid for, and the custom candy and decorations had been delivered to his dad's house. I also sent Tom with envelopes labeled "You are now at (insert place) at (insert time). Open this envelope," and inside each envelope was the appropriate receipt, schedule of events, his to-do list, guest list, phone numbers, a hand-drawn layout of where to put the decorations, the candy, etc. as well as a written speech for each event. Tom called this his "wedding planner in a suitcase" and said he would have given me a five-star recommendation, had I "still been in business."

We planned to name this baby Thomas Andrew but would call him Andy for short. T-A names are a tradition in Tom's family, and Andrew was after my hero, Andy. Tom would speak to the baby via my belly button, which he jokingly called the "baby's cell phone." This little embryo had made a place in our hearts and home from the very minute he was placed inside my uterus. I knew I was pregnant within days of the frozen embryo transfer (FET) of the first viable embryo: I was exhausted, my dreams were vivid, my boobs were huge, and I couldn't look at food. My symptoms were so awful that we were elated, and I was so happy every time I threw up, so much so that we went straight out to buy a stroller we'd been eyeing and also some other random baby items, then went to a baby consignment store and purchased more items we would eventually need. On the Wednesday before Tom left town, we went to one of my favorite restaurants so I could get my favorite soup, chicken tortilla, which we felt was something I would eat no matter what, and I spent the entire dinner in the bathroom eating saltines! I didn't get my favorite soup, and I left the restaurant grinning from ear to ear.

That Friday, I got a nasty call about collections on a lab bill that was billed incorrectly. The lady on the phone yelled that I was irresponsible and trying to get out of paying a bill. Try as I might, she would not let me speak. Finally, I just yelled back, louder and angrier than I had yelled before, so that I could speak over her. Within minutes I felt cramping, but figured it was just because that call took a lot of energy out of me, and I lay down. Nine days post transfer, on August 7th, 2016, and with Tom back in town, I went for my blood draw and stopped for bagels on the way home while we anxiously awaited the hCG results. My hCG level came back at 3.5. The doctor said this meant that I did conceive but something happened. I begged the doctor to recheck in 72 hours; maybe the embryo just had a delayed implantation. While he didn't feel this was late implantation, he did agree to retest in 72 hours. That Monday we did another blood test and my hCG was zero.

The doctor called this a chemical pregnancy, which meant I was pregnant but lost the pregnancy before the pregnancy was seen on ultrasound. I felt this loss, I felt guilt and thought it was my fault, I grieved, and then I thought, "Maybe this doesn't count because it was a chemical pregnancy?" but it did. This was a miscarriage. This was a loss. Not only did I lose the embryo that started to grow and develop inside me, I lost hope, I lost the future I hoped and planned for with this baby, I lost our Thomas Andrew and I lost a piece of my heart that was reserved for this baby. Every loss counts. No matter how big or how small, a pregnancy or something other, a loss is a loss. Having this realization, I finally let myself feel and I let the guilt go.

In between losing Andy and our next FET, I had knee surgery numbers two and three and also obtained my real estate license.

On Wednesday, March 15th, 2017 we proceeded with another embryo transfer, a girl we would call Tandy Lynn. Tandy combined Thomas Andrew and Lynn is my middle name. The transfer went well, but the likelihood of her implanting was smaller than the boy as her embryo grading was lower. I never got any of the symptoms that I felt with Faith and Andy, but I tried to stay positive and calm. Tom "called" her every night and sang. I rubbed my belly as often as I could and also sang the "wash baby" song in the shower that I sang with all my pregnancies: "wash, wash, wash the baby, rub, rub, rub the baby." Tom answered all phone calls this time and I incubated while trying to grow a real estate business from the couch.

The blood test was on March 24, 2017, our 10th anniversary, and for our anniversary, two of our beloved friends gifted us with tag-teaming Faith and her crazy weekend schedule so that we could go off for the weekend. After dropping Faith at school and her duffle bag with the friend that would take the first 24-hour shift, we went to the doctor's office for the blood test and then headed out for our road trip to Las Vegas. For the first half of our trip we talked about life with a newborn and two girls. We discussed our strategy for winning at the casino so that we could pay for all the prom gowns, cars for 16-year-old girls, two college educations, and three weddings. We were excited, and the project manager in me wrote a financial plan for the future in an email (to us) on my phone.

Somewhere in the middle of the desert without any phone reception, the doctor's office called and left me the voicemail. Tandy Lynn did not implant. I got the message on the other side of 'no-signal-somewhere-in-the-desert land.' Tom had to pull over; he was too sad and couldn't drive through the tears. My heart broke again. The breath felt stuck in my throat and I felt as if I couldn't breathe. I called the nurse back and questioned whether her message was correct ("yes"), had she gotten the test results mixed up with someone else's ("no"), can we retest ("no"). She suggested that we look at our options again after we'd had some time to sit with this and make peace with the outcome and perhaps after I lost 50 pounds.

Not only was I destroyed emotionally, but now I felt inadequate in my own skin. The focus for the rest of our road trip was finding quick ways to lose weight. I already had the answer but hoped for a weight-loss magic wand. As Tom drove and I became more and more frustrated with not finding a quick way to lose 50 pounds. My thoughts changed to "how are we supposed to have a fun anniversary weekend in Las Vegas?" How could we possibly enjoy ourselves now? I was afraid to eat or drink or do anything that would cause me to consume extra calories. With each thought I felt less and less like me and more and more like someone filled with sadness, questions of why, and embarrassment about her own skin. When we finally made it to our hotel, my eyes were so swollen from crying that seeing was difficult and I ended up making an unexpected trip to the salon to get eye cream and of course let them sell me on "feel pretty" products because at that moment it was what I needed. Tom and I did our best, and we did enjoy our weekend away because we were together. We were able to hold each other, talk for endless hours, see a few shows, toast our anniversary, and get wedding ring tattoos, and I made sure we got our 10,000 steps in a day so I could enjoy myself without "worry." Driving back, reality hit us both hard.

People would shame me when I spoke of Tandy as a loss; to most, Tandy never came to be, she did not stick. Therefore, why cry and grieve something that never was? If I had a penny for every time in my fertility journey that I heard, "At least it happened early" or "Tandy just wasn't meant to be," "You should be glad that you lost Andy early, before you could get attached," I could rule the world with all the pennies.

I was consumed with guilt and sadness. I felt in my heart that these outcomes were because of me, my weight, my body, the consequences of my actions. I could list 50 different ways to blame myself, one for each pound I needed to lose. I wasn't receiving the support that I needed because I was surrounded by people who didn't understand infertility, and that's okay, they were still good friends. However, I also needed to surround myself with people who understood, people who were on a similar journey. Life isn't meant to be lived in darkness or silence but treasured in the light. I had to make a conscious decision to rid my life of toxic things, including people, even though this meant not having parties and a busy social schedule. This didn't mean that I was choosing a life of solitude or darkness; this was my way of seeking people that lifted me up instead of pulling me down, and I did. I am a true believer that God removes people from your life to create room for the people who you do need.

I later came to learn that I had a fibroid in my uterine wall, and where the fibroid was located, it likely left no room for the embryo to firmly attach. None of this was my fault. There was nothing I could have done to cause the fibroid. The losses weren't my fault either.

I found my strength in the dark when I refused to sit back and listen and instead found the strength and accepted responsibility for my own health, actions, and outcomes, which I did by searching for the answers to my recurrent losses. This strength was buried deep down under a lack of belief and fear of the answers. I have a voice and I let it go silent. Please don't lose your belief in the power of you, please don't let fear take over your heart and your actions. I believe in each one of you as much as I believe in myself, and if needed, please borrow my belief until you can believe in you on your own.

Do you remember in Chapter 3 when the doctor joked with Tom about installing a light switch during his vasectomy reversal? What if we install a dimmer switch in ourselves (not literally of course) so when our light goes out, we can turn the lights back on a little at a time. I view my strength as a dimmer switch: some days the light is dim and I don't feel strong, and other days the light is turned all the way on and I feel powerful. The dimmer switch doesn't have to be steady; after all, we are humans and we are dealing with life. For me finding strength in the dark happened when I realized and accepted that not every day is going to be my best, most amazing, brightest light day, and that is 100% OKAY as long as I know where the dimmer switch is to bring the light and not let the light go all the way out.

CHAPTER 8

IT WASN'T MY FOREVER; IT WAS MY RIGHT NOW

I remember, like it was yesterday, the second time I hurt my knee. I was 15 and performing on stage, wearing a zoot suit with slicked back hair, dancing to "Vogue" by Madonna. I went down on my knee (as choreographed) and missed the next eight count because I couldn't get up. I left that performance and went straight to the emergency room. The ER doctor diagnosed me with a sprained knee and put my knee in brace that immobilized my leg from the thigh to my calf, with crutches, for a month. The only good thing that came from that is I got to use the school elevator vs. the crowded staircase and was moved to adaptive PE vs. regular PE. In the world of teenage drama, I was devastated because my boyfriend had brought his family to watch and meet me and broke up with me because he was embarrassed. My pediatrician felt that my knee was doing better, so I moved on with life; however, my knee was a problem from that point on, always swollen, always hurting, but I managed. I was in an adaptive physical education class where I spent the hour doing exercises to strengthen my knee.

In November 2008 I was watching TV with Jonathan in our sunroom and got up to get drinks. While I was walking from the sunroom into the kitchen, my knee bent backwards and collapsed. Jonathan was grossed out. Tom took me right to the orthopedic doctor who did an MRI and diagnosed me with a torn meniscus, which he planned to repair on November 25th. The doctor told me it was a simple surgery and I would be able to make Thanksgiving dinner on the 27th.

I woke up from surgery and the nurse brought Tom in. After he kissed me and I was able to keep my eyes open, he said, "Do you want the bad news or good news first?" I said, "Give me the bad news first," and he did. "The bad news is your knee is broken, but the good news is your knee is fixed." Is anyone else confused by that? I know I was. It seems that my knee was much worse than the doctor expected and the knee cap was blocking the damage on the MRI. I had no cartilage; the last bit of cartilage was hanging on for dear life. The doctor did a procedure that would, when I recovered, replace my cartilage with scar tissue. In the meantime, I was absolutely non-weight baring for six weeks and partial for another eight and would likely need a knee replacement in three years, as this was considered a band-aid fix. On the way home Tom said, "There's more bad news." More, seriously! He said, "You can't cook Thanksgiving dinner. You need to stay in bed." That was the Thanksgiving that people brought Thanksgiving to me and we ate in our master bedroom with me lying in bed and a card table set up for everyone else. I did my physical therapy, and my knee hurt a lot, but over time I learned the things I could do. I guess the experience was bad enough, though, that people got to know my knee more than me. I was told by a lady at church, "I don't know your name but I know your knee." With time I learned to do the things I could not do because of my knee, and the things I could do, like live a happy life, and I didn't have a knee replacement three years later.

In 2016, my knee was in really bad shape. We were afraid that I had taken my knee as far as I could. That year I had two surgeries before ending with a total knee replacement in 2017, at 41 years old. The doctor realized it was time when he couldn't scare me about what life would be like with a metal knee. What is it with me and surgeries during the holidays, but guess when I had it? Yep, you're right. That November. But at least this time it was after Thanksgiving. Jonathan brought his wife, Liza, to California, and Patti came out for a visit too, and I made dinner for five. Surgery was on November 29th, 2017. I remember being wheeled into the OR, and as they were getting me onto the OR table, I looked to my right and saw the saw and drill and looked to the left at the anesthesiologist, and said, "Now! Now would be a good time to put me under!" The next thing I remember is waking up in the recovery room. That first night was rough because I was in a lot of pain. The next day would be spent with physical therapy so I could go home that afternoon. The first PT round was hard, but I was able to use a walker and get around. I didn't get to do the second PT round, though, because my blood pressure was too low, which also meant I was not going home that day.

Tom and Faith came to visit me later that evening, and I wasn't responding to him or Faith. He called for the nurse, who had just started his shift. He said I was probably just sleeping because of pain meds, only my eyes were open. He checked and I hadn't had pain medicine since the morning because my blood pressure was too low. Tom said that he tried to stimulate me and I didn't respond. As Tom told me the nurse called a code and the code team, maybe a few more than 10 people, came running in, pushing both Tom and Faith into the corner. By this time, I was responsive and scared; the team quickly pushed my bed down to CT, telling Tom that it looked like I had a stroke. I spent the next four days in the critical care step-down unit, being monitored. When I was able to walk up and down stairs without my blood pressure being too low and was cleared by cardiology, neurology, and the ortho surgeon, I was sent home. Tom had a hospital bed waiting for me in the living room, speech therapy came to see me two to three times a week, physical therapy was visiting daily, and I had a home health nurse come once a week to check my blood pressure and draw blood. While I was still very confused, and at times had a hard time remembering Tom and Faith's names, I was home where I needed to be and the best place to recover.

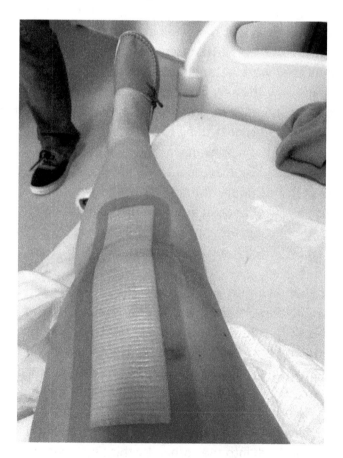

I felt better, so Tom went back to work and things were settling down. On December 21st I wasn't feeling well most of the day, and in the afternoon, I was shaking, I called Tom and my speech was garbled. He told me to call the neighbor and have her take me to the ER, where he would meet me. When I got to the ER, they immediately called in the stroke team, who rushed me through all the tests and into an ER room. I didn't have a stroke, but something wasn't right. My white blood cell count was 27,000. I was diagnosed with sepsis and the ER doctor felt the infection was coming from my knee. I was discharged on December 24th after being hooked up to IVs and machines. The source of the infection was never found, and although the sepsis diagnosis was still valid based on other tests and symptoms, the doctors never found an infection. Nobody could explain what happened, only that my knee wasn't infected.

Tom hosted our annual Friendmasukah party (where we get together with all of our friends and celebrate each other's holidays) on the 23rd; I didn't want him to cancel for Faith's sake, so he hosted all by himself. I felt broken laying in that hospital bed. I started to cry uncontrollably and the nurse called in the chaplain, who provided some comfort, and with his help I was able to stop crying. But I still felt broken. This was the most emotional and physically exhausting recovery. I was sad for Faith, the trauma that she must have felt being pushed to the corner while watching all these people work on her mommy and then having to put on protective equipment to visit me in the hospital but not being allowed to touch me. I can't even begin to imagine how Tom felt, watching all of this happen to his wife. The fear he must have experienced. I was scared. Scared for me. Scared for my family. Would I ever fully recover?

I was home for Christmas, and the hospital bed would be picked up in two days. While in the hospital, I got to work with PT and when I left, I was using a cane and not a walker. I was upstairs lying next to Tom, and on the same floor as Faith. The only thing I could do at this point was fight my way back. I had to fight harder than I ever had in my life, and I had to do it for my baby girl, Faith, and my amazing husband, Tom. I had to do it for myself. I went for physical therapy three times a week, I went for walks outside, and I lifted weights at home. I cleansed my body of all toxins and I started following an anti-inflammatory diet with only whole, clean, organic foods. As soon as I was able, I joined an exercise gym and worked out with a personal trainer.

I found my strength in the dark when I realized that what I was experiencing at the time would be my right now, NOT my forever. I stopped feeling sorry for myself and found a way to be stronger than the pain. The orthopedic surgeon had told me that this would be my knee for the next 20-30 years, and it would be the knee I would make it be. He said if you want to really live life again, then make this knee "your *itch," and I did. He said I would never run again, but I ran. He said I would never ride a bike again, but I did. He said I would need to give up dancing, and, no, I didn't listen to that either. He said I would never wear high heels again, but did you see the cover? I like a challenge. Tell me no and watch what I can do to tell you YES!

CHAPTER 9

VEGAS OR BUST!

11 years on March 24, 2018. Tom and I had been married for 11 years (already), and after all we had been through, we decided for our 11-year anniversary we would renew our vows. We had so much to celebrate and so much that would come, and after all we just grew through, we both knew it was time for Tom and Annette 2.0. Eloping in Vegas has always been a dream of mine, and Tom said yes!

I wanted to be vintage Hollywood glam for our second wedding and picked out a "vintage" tea-length wedding dress with lots of lace and fluff, complete with hot pink Mary Janes with heels, a (fake) fur stole and the glitziest fake jewelry I could find. Wearing heels of any height is not something I had done in quite a while because of my knee but something I really wanted to do to kick off "US 2.0," and as a backup I ordered satin pink "vintage" tennis shoes. When both pairs of shoes arrived, the first thing I did was hide them (along with the dress) from Tom. Each day I would take out the pink heels and stare at them, and inside I was thinking, "These shoes are going to be my *itch." I would then proceed to put them on. Starting slowly, I would put them on and just wear them while sitting at my desk. Two weeks before the big day I started practicing walking in them. I felt like I was experiencing heels for the first time and even stumbled. My foot and leg had been swollen since the surgery, so honestly the heels hurt, but I was not going to let pain control or define me. I kept at it and was determined to wear the shoes walking through the hotel to my Froggy Bear and down the aisle and in pictures, and I would get my foot-popping kiss at THIS wedding.

Being that it was our wedding, we flew out to Las Vegas first class from Los Angeles, we wore matching shirts that said "We Still Do," and due to a misfortunate incident in Vegas on our prior anniversary the hotel upgraded us to a LUXURY suite, at no additional charge. We had an amazing time in Vegas; we went to shows, ate wonderful food, sat and watched Vegas go by while cuddling up with each other. We talked! We talked so much, and after nearly 13 years of being together, we discovered new things about each other. Our trip was a honeymoon both before and after our ceremony. We connected on so many levels that we did feel that the ceremony was not our fresh start; this reconnection was our fresh start. This trip, only 300 miles from home, had become the trip of a lifetime, more so than our actual honeymoon in the Dominican Republic.

We had a few friends come in for the event, and after sitting by the pool, it was time to get ready and take these shoes out on the town. I had my hair and makeup beautifully done, and when I put my dress on, the reality of how much food and wine we had that weekend came crashing down! My friends tightened the corset even more as I sucked it in even more. Now I knew how a real vintage bride felt, complete with "I am okay as long as I don't breathe." I left the suite, walked down the long hall, standing in the elevator and stopping along the way so that random strangers could take pictures (by request) with a FREAKING HOTTTT BRIDE. The reality is that a Vegas bride is a tourist attraction, and they would have asked me for a picture even if I had a big ol' green zit on my nose (the zit was on my chin and triple concealed), and the other truth was that my HOTTT shoes were super slippery on the carpet because I hadn't scuffed the bottoms up, and I was doing everything I could to not be the bride laid out on the floor in a pile of fluff. It took me about 10 minutes of slipping and sliding to finally get to my Froggy Bear. I tapped him on the shoulder and his jaw dropped, literally. Our sparkly gold limo was outside waiting to take us, and our friends, to the chapel.

Tom was taken into one room and I was ushered to the bride's room to wait for our number to be called, like in the deli department at the grocery store: "Now serving number 72." I started to panic. Not only was the chapel live streaming the ceremonies on social media and their website, but we had paid extra to have a special live stream for our family and friends across the country AND Faith was my maid of honor on live stream back home, watching in her basketball uniform for her favorite basketball team with Tom's mom. We sent her a corsage and brownie mix as a total surprise.

As the ceremony started I went into complete and total panic, not because of marrying Tom but because I was about to walk down the aisle to my honey for our fresh start wearing shoes that (as silly as it sounds) represented our fresh start, and I was fearful of what it would mean for our fresh start if I didn't make it down the aisle. The doors opened and the panic stopped and my confidence set in. I was a survivor and so was Tom, and I was marrying my best friend, my soul mate and lover for life. I kept my eyes on my soon-to-be 2.0 husband and walked down the aisle with the biggest smile. We were married again by reciting our vows, the vows we wrote for each other. When it was time to kiss, I held my finger up to indicate "One moment, please," took as deep of breath as my corset would allow, and let the breath out. I (literally) grabbed Tom's face and pulled him in for a long, not-chapel-appropriate kiss and at the same time popped my foot. We proudly walked back up the aisle, took Vegas pictures, and took pictures with my friend holding her phone up so Faith could be in some of them. The tennis shoes came out for our reception back in the hotel's tequila bar and then playing black jack in the casino with our friends. When it was time to go home, we were ready. We had already been through grief, trauma, tragedy, financial strain, and a cross country move, and we were stronger than ever and ready to take on whatever else life threw at us. We had married 11 years prior as Mr. and Mrs. Pearson, and we left Vegas as the freaking Pearsons ready for whatever.

Our Vows

Mine

11 years ago, had we written our vows, here is what mine would have said: "I feel like everything in my life has led me to you. My choices, my heartbreaks, my regrets, everything, and when we are together my past seems worth it" (anonymous). If I had taken the job in Hawaii or Goldsboro, I would never have met you. But my heart knew better and was pulling me towards Raleigh NC because the heart knows best. My love for you and the vows I said in 2007 have so much more meaning today.

Don't worry all of that still applies but there is a 2.0!

No matter what challenges we have faced, we faced them together. The love between us has truly become one of the greatest love stories I have ever known. In fact, it's my favorite love story!

Over 12 years ago when we met, we began to write our story. We discovered the lessons our fairy tale would teach, we found good characters, and evil characters inserted themselves; we created an element of magic and we leaped over the obstacles together. The characters (us, BTW) in our story were strong, united, deeply in love, and best friends. Our lesson was that love conquers all, love grows deeper each day, love is united, love does not give up.

Our story has boldly said to the world that while our love story may not be perfect or the story others may want for us, and there may be varying opinions about villains and magical characters and the obstacles we climbed, our love story will live happily ever after. This is our love story! There is a saying written by Island Girl in 2019, "Forget about prince charming. Go for the Wolf. He can see you better, hear you better, and eat you better," and I would add, the wolf doesn't need to put a shoe on every girl in the kingdom to find you. Thank you for being my wolf (this is not free advertising for North Carolina State, BTW. Go Tarheels!!!)

I view our successes, failures, weaknesses, our sickness, our health, our periods of richer (and I am still waiting for the damn lottery check) and poorer to be a road that we travelled to get us to where we are today, with a deeper love, commitment, and passion for our marriage. We have been able to forgive each other, to console each other, to be each other's best friends and soul mates.

So, standing in front of you today, this is my **vow 2.0.**

In front of God, our family and friends, our children on earth and in heaven, tonight I promise:
To be your best friend
To be your life partner
To be your continued faithful partner
To feel blessed every day that I am married to my one true love, to be married to my wolf (AKA Froggy Bear)
I promise to encourage you

I promise to inspire you
I promise to love you truly through the storms
I will forever laugh with you, support you and depend on your entertainment during commercials
I promise to lift you up when you are down
I promise to laugh when you become a frog
I promise to remind you daily of your legal obligation to tell me I look pretty, to laugh at my jokes and tolerate that I will be outside of the house in pajamas
I promise to love you unconditionally
I promise to always draw hearts with my finger on your hand during church
I promise to love you
I promise to grow old with you
I promise to always be your co-partner in life, in our adventures, RV trips, bingo hats and do that thing you like me to do so much....
Until death do us part

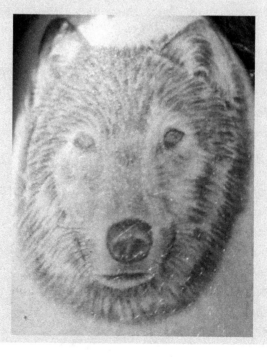

Tom's Vows

I knew you were special even before our first date from the long hours we spent chatting and emailing. The fun of that first date just confirmed what I already knew, that you are someone that enjoys life and would be a great friend, and hopefully more. As we dated, the romance and love grew as we experienced life together, both the good and bad. That first year proved that you would stand by me and support me even as life threw obstacles in our way. Instead of those obstacles breaking us apart they brought us closer together, culminating in our marriage 11 years ago today. On that day I married the woman who had become my best friend and companion, the other half of my heart. If someone had asked me on our wedding day if my love could grow stronger, I would have declared it impossible, and I would have been wrong. The last 11 years of celebration and love, struggle and disagreements, have made my admiration and love of you grow to ever greater heights, and the years have made me understand how lucky I am to be married to my best friend. When we are separate it is like I am missing part of myself, and I am only whole again when you are back by my side.

Annette, I look forward to keeping you by my side in the years to come as we face our future full of happiness and sadness, celebrations and trials, together as best friends, companions, lovers, and husband and wife. I give myself to you for the rest of our lives, dedicated to you and our love.

You see, these shoes, to me, symbolized that I had overcome the trauma my body faced. They represented the strength I had developed. To me these pink shoes were much more than a pair of high-heels; they represented the strength I found in the dark. I walked down the aisle on my own, wearing the type of shoes I was told I would never wear again, just four months later. I found my strength in the dark when I was told no but found a way to yes! I said no to the life people told me I would live and said yes to my dreams, my plans, and my life. I found my strength when I said boldly, "This is my right now, NOT my forever." Are you able to say that? I am not saying this is easy; I have to remind myself of this every day. It's one of my affirmations: What happens today doesn't have to be my forever, just my today.

Oh, by the way, I am pretty sure my Barbie had these same shoes, but she would have never worn the tennis shoes. Guess I have a few things now that Barbie doesn't have: 1) I am proud to be me and create my own style, 2) I am not plastic and neither are my shoes, and 3) my husband did not come in a box.

CHAPTER 10

MAYBE BABY, TAKE 4!

Before leaving for Vegas we made arrangements to begin our fourth and final IVF cycle; our first was with Faith in 2009. We had already spent over $200k going into the fourth procedure, and we knew we still had a long and expensive road to pregnancy. However, we figured coming back from our honeymoon all relaxed would be the perfect time to make magic happen, in the ultra-romantic fertility lab.

In preparation for cycle four, I exercised every day, I ate only organic foods, no soy, no gluten, no MSG, allergen free, no alcohol, and I cleansed my body. I was 42, and just like with the heels, I was strong enough to rock this cycle. Nothing was going to get in my way. I made sure my mindset was one of positivity, strength, and confidence. I felt confident in me, confident in my body. Whatever it was though, the doctor said that my egg production for cycle four was more than they could expect from a 20-something egg donor. Out of the 49 mature eggs, we produced 14 embryos, of which four were viable. Based on my age and previous outcomes, the doctor warned us that our statistics were in the upper 30th percentile, and then with each stage he was blown away because our statistics continued to increase and our outcome was looking more and more promising. We continued to deposit his words into our confidence bank and we began shopping for a large SUV. We went from not being able to give Faith a little brother or sister to being able to give four younger siblings. I would be the oldest mom on the soccer field pushing a four wide stroller and that seemed perfect.

With the knowledge that I had this fibroid and the possible impact it had with Andy and Tandy, my doctor wanted to do an MRI to check for location before we proceeded with any additional transfer cycles. I went for the MRI, and sure enough the fibroid was protruding into my uterus and would need to be removed before we could proceed with our next cycle. The surgery was called a myomectomy, which is a surgery to remove uterine fibroids. Ugh, anesthesia again?

The doctor sent me to see a gynecologist who specialized in laparoscopic pelvic surgery. While any gynecologist could do this surgery, the concern was the approach; most would do this as a major surgery requiring a lengthy hospital stay with possible impact to fertility and put me at risk of having a hysterectomy. The doctor I was being referred to had a proven record for success. After looking at my MRI results or what Tom and I began to call "Pictures of Thelma the one-eyed alien," he agreed that we needed to proceed with surgery, which was scheduled for two weeks later. The doctor reported that I actually had two fibroids, the first was Thelma and the second was her cousin, Ingrid, who was sitting right on my fallopian tube, and that between the six weeks of the MRI and surgery, Thelma had grown and was now the size and weight of a 14-week fetus, which answered why nothing fit me anymore. I stayed in the hospital overnight for pain control and went home to recover. Although I only had three minor incisions on my stomach, I had 24 stitches in my uterus. The recovery was equated to that of a c-section.

I was given a window of four to six months until we could resume fertility treatments. During this time, I focused on my mindset and continued with healthy lifestyle changes. In reality I thought, "After going through this surgery and recovery I HAVE to conceive, otherwise what was it all for?" My mindset clearly had to be shifted because that was clearly stinking thinking that had no place inside of me. Time to evict those thoughts because they had not paid their rent. These thoughts were only creating anxiety and negative energy, which could undo all the positivity and healthy lifestyle transformations that I had made. So anytime I had thoughts like "It's not going to happen," "The surgery was for nothing," "I can't do this," or "I am not strong enough," I first acknowledged the thought and then also acknowledged the reverse: "This is going to happen, I need that bigger car," "The surgery was needed for everything," "I can and I will do this," "I am not only strong enough, I am enough," and I gladly welcomed the positive thoughts into the penthouse at a rent discount because I knew they would be good tenants. Sometimes a mindset shift comes from us tricking our brain, and to anyone that might say, "You're talking to your brain?" feel free to sarcastically respond, "You can hear inside my brain? That takes a different kind of skill."

"Tell the negative committee that meets inside your head to sit down and shut up."
~ Ann Bradform

We started our cycle in October 2018, but the cycle was called off on October 12th because my uterine lining had stopped growing. Perhaps it was still too soon after the surgery. Even with all the positivity I have just shared, the lights started to dim, and I started letting all the negativity back into my heart. The doctor prescribed a few tablets of an anxiety medication, Tom took the rest of the day off of work, and we spent the day holding each other through the tears and together shifting our mindset from negative to positive, which took work and creativity, but we knew it was a must. Faith would be home from school soon and we couldn't let her see or sense our disappointment, and we knew most importantly we had our Faith, and she would be coming home with gigantic bear hugs and a huge smile.

You know how "they" say everything happens for a reason? On October 8th I had just dropped Faith off at school and was on my way home to work (I work from home) sitting at a stop light when I was rear-ended not once, but twice. Faith was out of the car for maybe three minutes. Thank goodness she was safe at school. I was badly injured. My grandma told me all the time as a kid, "Don't leave the house without clean panties." Guess what? I ran Faith to school in Tom's boxers (without panties), a hoodie, and my house slippers. Tom rushed from work over 20 miles away and was at the accident scene in 25 minutes. I didn't ask any questions. I asked him to please take me to the ER instead of the ambulance because of what I was wearing. I shouldn't have been at that time, but I was embarrassed, and I also didn't want my slippers in the dirty ambulance. I am sure anyone addicted to wearing slippers will understand, and the rest of you feel free to laugh.

At the ER I had a bruise on my neck and partial rupture in my lung from the seat belt tightening. I also had a lot of swelling and bruising on my back. I was sent home with pain medicine, a neck collar, and strict instruction to rest for the next 72 hours or until I could see my primary care doctor. I prayed to express gratitude to God for protecting Faith by having this happen after she got out of the car and also for protecting our embryo. The doctors would have given me a choice of treating me at the risk of miscarriage or not treating me, and I clearly needed the treatment. In this instance two things happened for a reason: Faith was at school safe and had no idea the ambulance and fire department were there for her mommy, and I didn't need to make the awful choice to be treated or not. I also prayed for the blessing of being able to develop my mindset so I could see the miracles that happened on October 8th.

When I was at home resting and that next evening, I started shaking and shivering, and I couldn't get warm. Tom took my temperature and it was 102.9. He decided to call for an ambulance. Thankfully Faith was at dance so, again, she wouldn't have to see this happening to her mommy. The ambulance got to our house, and I couldn't get down the stairs. My heart rate was 166 and my fever was now approaching 104. With full lights and siren and Tom following closely, I was taken to the hospital. Immediately I had multiple IVs, a heart monitor, and cooling blankets with my temperature nearing 105. The doctors said that I was septic, with a white blood count of 33,000 and they weren't sure why I was septic. The day before my white blood cell count was mildly elevated and now it had sky rocketed. The doctors never found out what caused the reaction. I was septic by symptoms, but just like the last time, every lab test performed for an infection came back negative. I was released three days later not knowing what happened or why, and still needing treatment for my back and neck, but everything else had returned to normal. A few months later I came to know that I have a condition called Reactive Leukocytosis, which causes my white blood cells to rise and try and attack any inflammation or trauma in my body. I went home and focused on recovery, my daughter, and my husband, and in November we resumed fertility treatments.

I found my strength in these dark moments when so much around me was negative and I looked for the positive. Yes, I was in a bad car accident, but I recovered. Thankfully, I had spent a lot of time on my health before all this happened or things might be a lot worse. Everyday my beautiful daughter ran to me for hugs. She never stopped being my cheerleader, and I was still there to be her cheerleader. My husband was by my side every step of the way. The biggest positive? I didn't give up on myself, and I always believed in the power of me. I am enough.

CHAPTER 11

ARE YOU THERE, GOD?

Do you have a minute before we get into this chapter? This next chapter is powerful but may also bring tears. So, before you start please grab a comfy blanket, some tissue, and a beverage of choice. Please also remember the disclaimer at the front of this book. *This is my story and in no way is it meant to provide medical advice nor invoke doubt or fear nor become your story. Should you have any questions or concerns related to the topics discussed in this book, please contact your physician.* My hope remains that as I share my story you will focus on how I fought my way back physically, emotionally, and spiritually and that you will focus more on the strength and less on the pain.

The Story of Thomas Asher Pearson (Tommy)

In November 2018 the doctors had decided that even though I was still in physical therapy from the car accident, I had recovered enough that we could resume preparation for our next frozen embryo transfer (FET). We had four viable embryos remaining, and we planned to go in scoring order, regardless of gender. This cycle was so different because we did not have the lining issues we had previously. We were full steam ahead and on track for a December 11th transfer. I was very excited for this date, actually, because not only was I positive we would conceive but it would also be a wonderful present for Tom, and we would tell Faith by Valentine's Day.

The transfer went perfectly, and although there is no proven study that resting for five days post transfer would improve the chances of pregnancy, it worked with Faith and I wasn't going to take any chances. So, I took off from work and went back on Monday, December 17th. I had five glorious days of sitting on the couch watching Christmas movies and movies that made me laugh. While there is no proven study, I had read that keeping your feet warm and watching funny movies would improve chances of implantation. Do you remember all of the benefits of laughter from Chapter 1? I watched all the classics. Tom also stayed home so that I only got off the couch to use the bathroom and go upstairs for the night. I continually rubbed my belly and spoke to our little "emby," and Tom did too. We were already so much in love with this baby.

I went for my first pregnancy test on December 20th and went back to work after leaving the doctor's office. I tried hard to focus on work as I needed the distraction. There were very few people around as most had taken off for the holidays. I turned on the TV in my home office and tried to continue the distraction by watching reality TV. I kept looking at the phone, thinking I may have missed a call or maybe I wasn't getting cell service. Suddenly I got a text message from the nurse with a picture of my hCG results, and the text simply said, "OMG, the doctor hasn't even seen these yet, but I couldn't keep you waiting." I got the message loud and clear this time, I was pregnant!

I called Tom at work. "Hi, Honey," I said, and the roles changed. It was now Tom who didn't believe it.

Tom replied, "What's wrong, are you okay, what'd the doctor say?"

"Honey, I haven't heard from the doctor yet," I said. Tom sounded disappointed and asked if I could call the doctor for the results. "Honey, I don't need to call the doctor. I know the results," I replied.

"You do?" he said.

"Yes, we are pregnant. We are having a baby. Faith is going to have a baby brother!" I happily said. He didn't believe it until I sent him the text from the nurse, to which Tom responded "We're pregnant, Faith is going to have a baby brother, we are going to have a baby!" The doctor did call and was thrilled. At this point we had been his patient for over four years and he had never given up on us or stopped believing that we could get pregnant. When Tom came home, we held each other tight and he kissed me with such passion, and then he kissed my belly with tears in his eyes.

I went back in 72 hours and the numbers had increased but hadn't quite doubled, so there was a bit of concern; it might have been a timing issue or something might be wrong, but the doctor asked that we not be fearful until we get the next result. It was December 23rd and I would go back into the doctor the morning of the 26th before going to the infusion clinic. The doctor decided that this cycle he would treat me with two rounds of IV intralipids, one before the transfer and one within a week of a positive pregnancy test. The 26th would be my second infusion.

In my heart I wanted to remain positive, but my mind kept going towards, "Why am I here getting this infusion, not covered by insurance, when I may not even be pregnant?" and I had to work really hard to turn my negative thoughts into positives. Thankfully the clinic wasn't busy and I had a nurse who sat with me and talked me through the two hours to keep my mind in a better place. As the nurse was taking the IV needle out of my arm, the text message had come in: my hCG had more than doubled, so the result on the 23rd was just a timing issue. We were pregnant and the baby was healthy.

We packed up and went off on our camping trip to Chula Vista, CA, where my mom and stepdad would meet us, flying in from Chicago, and we'd stay together for a week. Along the way, Tom had to stop about every 50 miles for me to pee. Chula Vista is in the San Diego area, and we did not expect or prepare for San Diego to be as cold as it was in winter. We were freezing! We ended up leaving early because I got so sick, which turned into a sinus infection and bronchitis. Things were proceeding and the pregnancy was going very well. We were so excited, still not telling anyone for a few weeks. We started ordering things for the baby and preparing the room that would be the nursery. I counted down the days until our next ultrasound so I could check on baby Tommy. I was very encouraged that there was no bleeding. This had been my first pregnancy where I hadn't bled in the early first trimester, but even with how well things were going, I just couldn't let go of fear. This baby was part of our home, our hearts, our family, and of course I was singing the "wash baby" song in the shower. Our first OB ultrasound was on January 9th, 2019; we heard our boy's heartbeat, we saw it fluttering. It was the most beautiful sound, just like the sound of Faith's heartbeat. I cried tears of happiness. Without any words, I had just received reassurance that our family would be growing to a party of five. On the way home we sent Tommy's first picture to each of the grandmas and there were actual shrieks of excitement from each.

Feeling confident, Tom and I decided we would share the wonderful news with Faith the next day, Thursday the 10th. I dropped Faith off, and we planned a Mommy and Faith frozen yogurt date after school. Tom was going to surprise her and be there too, and we would tell Faith she was going to be a big sister. I came back home and was working when I felt some cramps but didn't worry too much as I knew cramps could often be growing pains. Tom agreed but told me to call him and let him know how I was feeling. I went and lay down. Feeling better, I got up to go back into my home office, and as I walked out of my bedroom and took just a few steps into the loft I felt warmth and a gush come out of me. I ran to the bathroom, pulled down my panties, and found a large clot of tissue. I called Tom and told him to come quick, I was bleeding.

Tom rushed home and ran upstairs. I was sitting on the toilet covered in blood with a second clot in my panties. Tom called the doctor's office and our doctor was off for the day, but they got us in urgently with another doctor. Tom put towels on the passenger side seat and the medical assistant led us right back into an examination room with a trail of blood following behind me and my pants and panties filled with blood. The medical assistant got me cleaned up and prepped for the doctor, and with a Chux pad underneath me I proceeded to bleed on the table.

The doctor came in and read our chart, and he asked that I not be too worried since we had a wonderful ultrasound the day before and then proceeded with the vaginal ultrasound. He was silent and his silence felt like it would never end, or maybe it was more that I didn't want it to end because that would mean the baby was okay. Eventually he turned the screen towards us and showed us what he was seeing. "Your uterus has so much blood in it I am not sure what I can see or not see, but I think there is a still a heartbeat right here." Tom saw it too and was assured. The doctor said the best plan was to go home and return on Sunday when our doctor would be in the office, and until then I should be on complete bed rest. With that he looked at us with long eyes and said, "Good Luck, call if the bleeding gets worse or if you feel light headed, and drink a lot of fluids." The medical assistant and nurse came in, and while the assistant was cleaning me up and wrapping me in a Chux pad for the ride home, the nurse went over a few instructions with us, basically repeating what the doctor said. Tom drove us home and I had already saturated the two Chux pads I was wrapped in and proceeded to leave a trail of blood through the garage, up the stairs, and into my bedroom, where Tom helped me lie down before he went to get supplies. I lay in the bed, holding onto my tummy, praying and feeling the blood just gush out of me. There was nothing I could do to make it stop.

When Tom got home, I had him help me to the bathroom to clean up. He sat me on the toilet and the worst gush yet came out. I remember saying to Tom, "I love you and Faith so much, please don't let her forget me, you are the love of my life." It felt like my heart jumped, and with that I lost consciousness. I don't know how long I was out for, and Tom says it could have been a minute or more. Before coming to I remember "seeing" a white cloudy sky with two hands extending down to me after being in a prayer position. I felt like I was reaching towards the hands, but the hands pushed me away, and I woke up with Tom shaking me, calling out my name and crying like I had never seen him cry before and I was covered in sweat. We held each other tight. He was afraid that I died, and honestly, I felt like I had died. Tom was taking me to the hospital, and my personal doctor was on his way into the hospital to see me.

If Tom had called for an ambulance, I would go to the hospital in our town and not the one where the doctor would be meeting me. He begged and pleaded with me to find the strength to get into the car. I had just lost consciousness but knew what I needed to do. One foot at a time with blood seeping out of me, I walked down the stairs, out the door, and to the car again leaving a trail of blood behind me. Tom had me hold on to the car so he could lay down towels. When the jumping feeling in my heart started again, I immediately said, "Honey, get me in the car now or I am not going to be able to do it."

Most of what you will read over the next few paragraphs is based on the little bit I remember, and what I have been told by Tom and the doctors. We were off to the hospital and I was in and out of consciousness for the duration of the ride. From what I remember and what Tom told me, Tom pulled up and called out to a security guard to bring a wheelchair. The security guards lifted me out of the car and onto the chair, wheeling me into the hospital. One of the guards grabbed a towel and covered up my lower half to give me a bit of privacy since my lap was covered in blood. The nurse asked for the reason of our visit, and Tom said, "She is pregnant and bleeding a lot." The nurse asked him how far along I was and Tom told her I was seven weeks. The nurse then told Tom to have a seat and they would get to me as they had time. Tom yelled back, "My wife lost consciousness, she is in and out of consciousness, she's bleeding a lot."

The emergency room doctor, in response to the yelling, came out to see what was going on. Tom told her that while I was only seven weeks pregnant, I had lost consciousness several times and I was having severe bleeding. The ER doctor took me back herself. With the doctor by my side, the triage nurse tried to get my blood pressure and wasn't able to get a reading, and my pulse was very low, while blood just continued to flow out of me and down the wheelchair. I was quickly wheeled back to the trauma room, leaving a trail of blood behind me. I came to with a nurse rubbing his fist with pressure on my chest and Tom saying my name again but also saying, "come on baby, I can't lose you," and I opened my eyes. I had IVs in both arms, both hands, and in my right shoulder so that the trauma team could push IV hydration. I was alert and my blood pressure was rising. I was in a lot of pain, which felt like the labor pains I had with Faith. The doctor ordered an ultrasound and there was no sac, no heartbeat, only an empty uterus. Our baby boy, Tommy, went to heaven that day on angels' wings and received a pair of his own.

My doctor met us at the hospital and after examining me, he rushed me into surgery for a D&C. The urgency of the matter required that other scheduled surgeries be pushed back. On the way into surgery the ER doctor stopped us and said that my cardiac levels didn't look good and it appeared that I had a heart attack. She was admitting me into the hospital, post-surgery. As I waited for the surgery suite with my doctor and a nurse by my side, I couldn't stop crying. I felt like it was my fault this happened, I had to have done something wrong, and the nurse kept assuring me that I did nothing wrong, she had just had a miscarriage a few weeks prior. My doctor stepped aside to speak with Tom about my cardiac level. Tom was crying too and the doctor just sat with him and comforted him until it was my time to go into the operating room.

I asked the nurse to hold my hand until I was under anesthetic, and she said she would and she would hold my hand all the way through. The nurses got me set up for the doctor as I bled on their gurney and on the OR floor. The nurse just kept holding my hand as I kept crying out loud, "My baby died and it's all my fault," and she would squeeze harder.

I woke up in the recovery room with Tom by my side and was then taken to my hospital room. A dear friend stayed at our house with Faith that night and kept her distracted and happy. She said that the blood was just that I was clumsy and spilled the ketchup I had for my chicken nuggets. I lay in that hospital bed in physical and emotional pain, feeling empty and numb. At 1 a.m. the floor nurse and blood transfusion team came into my room and started my first blood transfusion; they had been monitoring my hemoglobin and it had dropped significantly. I wish I knew whose blood I received because that blood kept me alive, and I would like to thank that person. The transfusion took a couple of hours, and then I was able to get some sleep.

That next day our doctor came to check on us during rounds. He sat and explained to us what had happened: I had a massive blood clot, which had opened up my cervix and I dilated. He did his best to help me understand that it wasn't my fault. No matter how much the doctor tried to explain, all I understood was that my body failed my baby boy. I was in disbelief and trying to understand what happened in the last 48 hours. It was just too much to absorb. We heard Tommy's heartbeat and it was strong and beautiful. We told our moms. I dropped Faith off at school and promised her a frozen yogurt date, and then she was picked up from school and taken to dance by our friend as I lay in a hospital bed with Tommy up in heaven, having had emergency surgery, being told I had a "runner's heart attack," and having been given one blood transfusion with another on the way. Surely this had to be a dream, right? I wanted to wake up and stop the dream, only I was awake and this was my new reality. Faith came to see me after school and came in just as I was getting the second blood transfusion. She was just happy to be with her mommy and I was happy to be with her. Faith discovered that she loves hospital meatloaf and declared that the hospital's meatloaf was better than mine and asked if they take "to-go orders."

We had to tell her what was going on. Surely, she had questions. I wondered if she was too scared to ask.

I said, "Faith, I want to talk to you about why I am in the hospital."

Faith replied, "Can we order more meatloaf?" Faith didn't want to know. She was scared; she had already been through so much. I started to cry.

Tom took over. "Faith, mommy had a baby in her tummy and the baby went to heaven yesterday." Faith cried and I held her tight, she then smiled and said, "Mommy and Daddy, don't be sad. God is going to give us a baby. Just pray, okay?" and with that she never cried again for Tommy, she just kept praying.

It felt good to be home again, but I couldn't go upstairs or into the garage. Although Tom did his best to scrub the carpet and clean the garage floor, there were still blood stains from the garage all the way up the stairs. We told Faith it was fruit juice that I spilled and she was confused because she was told it was ketchup.

I started therapy and was diagnosed with post-traumatic stress disorder (PTSD). I couldn't even use the master bath because that was where I lost our Tommy, that was where I met God, and that was all I could think about when I went near those places or when I looked at the stairs, and I would panic and cry ugly tears.

My primary care doctor sent me to a cardiologist and hematologist to monitor my follow-up care. The cardiologist wanted me to see the hematologist first because if my blood levels were not in a normal state it would impact my cardiac results. My hemoglobin, while better than before the last blood transfusion, was still low and so were my iron levels. He ordered weekly iron transfusions, and that's when I learned I am allergic to IV iron. Ha! I am quite the anomaly.

After receiving the clearance from all doctors, once again, I started to find my strength and take responsibility for myself and my care. I fully committed my heart to Christ and my mind to a healthy lifestyle. I turned my frustration into motivation and my sadness into drive. I pushed and challenged my body to do things I never thought possible. Having inflammatory arthritis, fibromyalgia, and a total knee replacement, surely, I had to defy all the norms and do more than wear pink heels. I joined kickboxing, starting with once a week, then twice a week, building my way up to twice a day. Despite Tom's hatred of exercise, I motivated him to join in and we passed a 250lb tank back and forth at the gym. I focused on healthy foods like protein shakes and allergen free, organic foods. I had gained so much weight during my physical and emotional recovery. My BMI decreased from 42% to 35% and I added 4% lean muscle in two months. My life was like those inspirational movie montages with a theme song that we see on the big screen.

We were ready to try again. We would never forget what happened, but we were going to move forward with our fresh start. First, we needed a pre-babymoon. Mom flew out from Chicago to stay with Faith so Tom and I could go on our first cruise. Of course, Faith was upset that she was not going with us, but we eventually were given her "permission" when we explained the cruise was just research so we could take her next time; we wanted to be sure we could tell her what to expect. With this agreement, we were instructed to send her videos and pictures of "everything." Our next frozen embryo transfer was scheduled for two weeks after our return, which seemed perfect. Perfect timing to make sure I still had a vacay-buzz. With our baby making medicine packed, we were on our way.

On the drive to the port, Tom confessed that he was nervous it wouldn't happen for us and scared that he would really lose me this time. It had taken a lot for Tom to be able to admit that to me. I had lost a lot of weight, I was healthy, and I really felt like this was our time. My response: "Honey, we have been through it all. This is our time and God is going to keep me safe. I will never leave you and Faith."

The cruise was amazing. We did our required "research," enjoyed being "off the grid," and even kept our healthy commitment to each other, but when we returned to Long Beach early before the sun came up, both of our phones started dinging like crazy. Welcome back to fire season (in California).

The Story of MaryGrace Hope Pearson

After spending nearly a year trying to understand why we lost Tommy and hearing "we don't know, we don't know" over and over and then committing ourselves to a healthy lifestyle, we, guided by faith, began the preparation for our next FET.

The day was here and I was nervous as could be, on my knees praying that I would keep my promise to Tom, that I would never leave him or Faith, and that the baby and I would be safe. Truth was that I was terrified that I would break both Tom and Faith's hearts again. That my heart would break again. Even on the drive there I was doing my best to turn my stinking thinking into positive words of wisdom to myself. Tom knew I was scared. He knew I was praying. I just didn't tell him why.

We had three remaining embryos and the doctor agreed to transfer two to improve our chances. We had discussed that if this transfer didn't "stick," we weren't sure we could go through a seventh. The doctor transferred one boy and one girl. "Please, oh please," I prayed, "Let at least one of these beautiful embryos be sticky and let my uterus be as sticky as fly paper." Early on I knew that this day would be the day that I would teach myself, again, about the beauty of God, patience, and determination, and I would learn this through one (or both) sticky embryo.

For five days I stayed in bed. Tom and I weren't taking any chances this time, and because we didn't want Faith to know, we told her I had the stomach flu. Faith's response: "Mommy, Daddy, I am nine, you can't fool me anymore. I know Mommy has a baby in her tummy," and we didn't confirm nor deny. I watched all of the best comedy movies from the 80-90s, and I wore one blue and one pink sock on my feet at all times to keep my feet warm. I was lazy for five days! I laughed for meditation, peace of mind, and good blood flow. Although it didn't take much to laugh, during the day Tom would hop around like a froggy bear, and Faith would come home with some funny story or "gossip" from the playground. On the seventh day all I wanted to eat was candy bars and everything else made me sick to my stomach.

I was scheduled to have my blood pregnancy test nine days after the transfer, and because there was a local fire, I wasn't able to go. Instead I pulled a two-year-old urine pregnancy test from my bathroom vanity, squatted, peed, placed the stick on the counter, ran out of the bathroom, and shut the door tight. Tom said, "Um, why did you close the door?" and I replied, "Because I don't want to take any chances of anything interfering with the test. So, let it cook and stay out here with me for 92 seconds." Tom immediately declared that I must be pregnant because I seemed to have lost my mind. Of course, he said it with more of a southern accent, like "You lost your mind!" Tom jumped up as soon as the timer went off, went into the bathroom, and screamed. I assumed this meant it was negative. He jumped out of the bathroom, "We're pregnant!" and I threw up. The nurse was excited and told me to come in the next day to have a blood hCG.

Faith didn't have school on the day of the blood test, so she would need to come with me. While we had dodged her "I know" statements before, I knew I had to get creative now. Faith had already figured out that all of the storks came from this doctor's office. I had told Faith we were just going to get a blood test to see how I was doing after the stomach flu. I almost had her convinced until the medical assistant said, "Congratulations, let's see just how pregnant you are." Are you kidding me? Faith's response: "Told you, Mommy. I am going to be a really good trauma surgeon." Not only was Faith very tall, sweet, brave, and smart, she also had my sarcasm and her dad's bad jokes. Several hours later we got the call, and I was very pregnant.

It was Halloween night. I wore a goat onesie, Tom wore a "grill," and Faith donned her favorite mythical character outfit. They went trick-or-treating, and I stayed home rubbing my goat belly, giving children way more candy than I should have because I was just so happy. I thanked God every day for this blessing, wondering if it would be twins.

When Tom and I were married for just a few months, we had adopted our first US dog. Bailey was allergic to dogs, so we had to adopt an allergen-free dog and we found the perfect four-month-old puppy, a chihuahua poodle mix known as a Chi-A-Poo. So that we didn't have any family arguments over the name, we each picked a name for our new puppy, Prince Fredrick Maxwell Mercury Pearson (four names from four people) and we called him Freddie for short. Freddie enjoyed tummy time and wearing dog clothes, he loved to be dressed and lie on a blanket with us all around him. Freddie even tolerated when we brought another puppy home, Tobiath Jr. or Toby, a Pekingese poodle mix known as a Pek-A-Poo. Freddie had a history of epilepsy and arthritis, but when he turned 14, he developed congestive heart failure.

Over the summer the doctor had put Freddie on meds and given him six months to a year even while taking the meds. Freddie refused to take the medicine. He would growl and show his teeth when we tried, and if we could manage to sneak the medicine into him, he would spit it out. The veterinarian said to just let him be in peace and stop the medicine. I was getting more and more worried, and I was able to tell that our puppy was really struggling. So, the day after Halloween we took Freddie to the vet, thinking she would tell us more of the same and we'd take him home. Instead we heard that his trachea was collapsing and he wasn't getting air. We were advised to put him down so that he didn't have a traumatic death at home. Something we weren't expecting at all. I picked out his urn and lit the candle in the office, which told everyone that a pet was going to heaven.

Faith and I hugged Freddie and told him we loved him. I thanked him for being the best puppy a puppy mommy could ever ask for and told Freddie who would be meeting him in heaven. I took Faith out to the car so we could cuddle while Tom stayed back with Freddie. Faith and I cried so hard and I held her as tight as I could. Tom and I had gone from celebrating to grieving in less than 24 hours. We weren't able to go home after; the thought of walking into the house without Freddie broke our hearts even more. Instead we decided we all needed retail therapy. We went out and bought our first (not family passed down) dining room table. It brightened the day to think that we needed a bigger table for a high chair and all the family that would be coming to see us.

As hard as it felt, we began to adjust to life without Freddie. At the same time, as the days went on, so did my morning sickness. Things were going well, until I started bleeding ten days after our positive test. This was about the same time I started bleeding with Faith, so I told myself (and Tom) not to worry. I was just going to have another complicated pregnancy and deliver a healthy baby or two. The doctor was reassured when we saw a sac and a fetal pole. Everything looked good, and he reminded me that bleeding could be expected in the first trimester, especially with my history. While the doctor saw a sac and fetal pole on the ultrasound for one baby, I saw the cutest little fish ever. I was glad to be the fishbowl, and we named the baby "fish." Tom made me stay on the couch and wouldn't let me do a thing, including taking Faith to and from school. Her school was maybe half a mile away, but he insisted.

A week later I passed a large clot and was heavily bleeding, my PTSD kicked in, and I had a panic attack. I couldn't breathe. Not again, please don't let this be happening. Tom took me to the emergency room, and we were so relieved to find out that the bleeding was another sub-chronic hemorrhage and we were able to see fish's heart beat for the very first time, beating at a strong 156 bpm. It took a few days for the bleeding to stop, and when we went in to the doctor we heard fish's heart beat for the very first time at 138 bpm. The doctor evaluated the sub-chronic hemorrhage and felt it was resolving. We were so relieved, and although I was still on bed rest, we were ready to celebrate a very thankful Thanksgiving. Tom's mom flew in from North Carolina to be with us.

Two days before Thanksgiving I was back in the emergency room. While lying down I felt a large gush of blood between my legs.

I tried to stay calm and remember what the emergency room doctor told me: "As long as it slows down and as long as you are not feeling lightheaded, rest and call your doctor." I couldn't rest, my PTSD was in full force, and this time so was Tom's. We tried to rest and see what happened, but the bleeding didn't seem to be slowing down and we were both scared. At 11:30 p.m. we went off to the emergency room.

Our experience was quite different this time. The doctor found a lot of blood around my cervix and blood flow in my uterus, and to their surprise, the radiologist, the emergency room doctors, my doctor, etc., none of them had seen anything like this before; however, since the heartbeat was strong at 153bpm, my hCG was rising to the appropriate levels, and they didn't see a sub-chronic hemorrhage, they sent me home on bed rest and very definitive instructions on when to return. Every day Tom, Patti, and Faith hung out with me. I worked (from bed) during the day. Tom and Patti made a cardboard table so we could eat and play games together as a family. Before leaving for work, Tom would bring up a cooler of all my pregnancy must-haves. We played a lot of cards, and just as Tom did while I was in labor with Faith, loved that I could not see everything going on being in a reclining position. I think it's because of the TLC and prayers, but we had a wonderful, thankful Thanksgiving without bleeding. Faith also enjoyed that this year she and her daddy got to cook dinner, and we ate dinner with me lying on the couch. Given that this would be Tom's first go at cooking Thanksgiving, I put on my project manager hat and wrote every detail out in a 30-page manual, titled "The Husband's Guide to Cooking Thanksgiving as Obsessively as His Wife." Coincidently, ever since the stroller issue, Tom has been very supportive of my need to obsessively plan.

After moving from North Carolina, I had found a wonderful OB/GYN doctor locally. She knew we wanted to expand our family and would do anything to help us but also knew that it would take a miracle for us to conceive naturally. She followed my care closely and was always rooting for us. After five years, we were FINALLY sitting in her waiting room for our first obstetrics appointment at nine weeks pregnant, the longest I had gone since being pregnant with Faith. I hadn't bled for two weeks, but we were finally at the doctor's appointment that we'd been wanting for five years, AND I came to the appointment spotting. The first thing she did was an ultrasound to show us our baby and also to check the bleeding. Fish was amazing and looked more and more like a teddy bear every day. This ultrasound was different because we saw fish wiggling and, as always, with a strong heartbeat. I couldn't see our fish smile yet, but I knew it was there. I felt fish's happiness in my heart and fishbowl. Fish had already changed our lives, all of ours. Faith was on cloud nine about being a big sister.

The OB then wanted to check for the blood flow in my uterus and cervix. She agreed it looked abnormal and said this was not going to be an easy pregnancy. Her assessment was that I probably had a vasa previa, a "rare condition estimated to impact one in 2,500 pregnancies...where some of the blood vessels are present in the membranes outside of the sac," according to the article "Vasa Previa Diagnosis and Treatment to Prevent Stillbirth" by Krissi Danielsson. If this was the case, then I could carry to 34 weeks and would require a C-section delivery, which I would have needed regardless because of the myomectomy. To confirm, our OB doctor wanted us to see a perinatologist as soon as possible, and we also scheduled NPIT genetic testing at ten weeks as I was considered a geriatric pregnancy at 43 years old. Our OB wasn't playing when she said as soon as possible; we saw the perinatologist two days later.

The perinatologist was very confused as to why we were seeing her so early in our pregnancy but proceeded with the visit. After scanning my fishbowl, she knew exactly why we came to see her. The perinatologist's assessment was that I had an adherent placenta, otherwise known as a placenta accreta, which is a "serious condition where the placenta grows too deeply into the uterine wall" (from the Mayo Clinic's article "Placenta accreta"). Suddenly the reason for my visit was clear and the perinatologist anticipated that if I chose to continue with this pregnancy, I would see her every other week through 34 weeks, when I would be delivered by C-section.

STOP!

"If you choose to continue this pregnancy"!

I heard that in my pregnancy with Faith. Of course I chose to continue this pregnancy! Yes, at just over nine weeks, the medical world still refers to a pregnancy as a first-trimester fetus; however, I refer to this and all my previous pregnancies, all pregnancies, mine or others', as the miracle of childbirth where we carry our baby that will grow and thrive in his/her "incubator" until the plug is pulled on their hot tub and our babies comes into this world to look lovingly at their parent(s), and in an instant everyone knows that moment was written in the stars. "Please," I prayed, "let my fish be healthy, safe, and held tightly in our arms to bless our home."

Tom and I boldly said, without hesitation and with strong intention, that we would without any doubt carry this pregnancy through to 34 weeks, when I would have a C-section and we would hold our baby in our arms.

A few days later I received a call from my OB.

"Hello."

"Annette," she said, almost dragging out my name with hesitation.

"Yes, hello, Doctor..." I said with so much anxiety.

"Annette, I saw the perinatologist over the weekend, and after reviewing your file with the other doctors in her practice," —insert long pause and sigh— "she is very concerned." The words were hard for her to say, and by the cracks in her voice I knew it wasn't going to get any better.

"Oh, I thought we had a game plan." I was doing everything I could to sound optimistic.

"Annette, a placenta accrete is very serious, and if not treated right you could die." This was followed by silence from us both for what felt like five minutes, but it was only 30 seconds. "Annette, I think you should consider termination." I heard the tears in her voice.

"No!" I said simply.

"Annette, you have a beautiful, healthy daughter here that needs you now. You have a wonderful husband that loves you so much," she continued.

"No! I have been down this road before with doctors that wanted me to terminate my pregnancy with Faith and she is here and she is amazing and wonderful and healthy and beautiful. No!" I said.

"Annette, if you choose to continue this pregnancy you will alternate seeing doctors every other week so you are seen weekly, and you will be on bed rest for a significant part of the pregnancy. The perinatologist wants to see you starting tomorrow."

"Great, I'll call her office now to make an appointment. Now can we talk about my yeast infection? It's annoying," and shortly after we ended the call.

I called over to the perinatologist's office. They had been waiting for my call and had an appointment scheduled for December 12th. I was ten weeks and one day into my pregnancy.

Unlike the first visit, at this visit she seemed to scan everywhere, and we even got a 3D image. A radiologist and ultrasound tech attended the appointment, too, to follow along and provide their thoughts. We received another confirmation that our fish was perfect, growing ahead of schedule (aha, the reason I was gaining weight), meeting or exceeding all milestones with a beautiful heartbeat. But as healthy as fish was the doctor could not forget what she was seeing with the placenta. The placenta was growing where it shouldn't be, and based on where the placenta had already been growing, there was concern that the placenta would grow through my uterine wall and towards my organs. The doctor told me to get dressed and we'd talk. From experience I know that when doctors say this it means something is behind the "get dressed and we'll talk," and in my life it hasn't been good things.

With the close of the curtain my tears started to flow, and so did Tom's. The doctor came back into the room and said, "It is my professional recommendation that you terminate this pregnancy as soon as possible. The risk to your health is too great." I knew right then that I would need to fight for this pregnancy, for my baby. I would need to fight with all I had because her life depended on it. Tom agreed but was still very worried about me, although he kept that to himself. We again said, "No! we are going to have our baby." At this point we were told that if our choice was to continue, then we would need to see a perinatologist at a university hospital as I could not get the level of care I would need locally. We understood her concern, but we also understood we had been down this road before, and it was a fight for us to get pregnant, and it would be a fight to deliver our healthy baby born from a healthy mama. If anyone was up for the challenge it would be us.

111

That night, Faith brought down a few stuffed animals so we could review "how to hold and swaddle a baby, how to change a diaper, and how to feed a baby." Just in case we were rusty, Faith declared herself to be the expert. When I pretended to give the stuffed animal a bottle, Faith simply responded with "I'll let that fly since this isn't our REAL baby, but you feed a real baby from your boobie." Yes, we were very confident with our decision. Our tadcub was ready to pass on her title and become a cub.

The next day while I was getting my blood drawn for the genetic tests, I received a phone call from the university hospital. "Annette, we'll see you at 1 p.m. today during the doctor's lunch." Faith was at school, and she expected to see us that afternoon, so we had to come up with a plan because we didn't want Faith to worry. Thank goodness for our neighbors. They picked Faith up and made a fun afternoon for her. We got the call at 10 a.m., and the hospital was 30 miles away from the lab, and although it was a pleasant drive, it took us over two hours to get to the hospital. Of course, Los Angeles traffic! We were at our appointment one hour early, which in the "suburbs" means you get in earlier, you are on your way home sooner, and the doctor gets lunch. Of course, in downtown Los Angeles an hour early means your chart doesn't get checked in until 15 minutes before your appointment time, and then you wait another two hours to be seen. The high-risk doctor at the university hospital confirmed the placenta issue but also said my suspected condition was so rare and that fish was so healthy that we should take this pregnancy week by week with the goal of a minimum of 24 weeks. The plan was at 24 weeks, I would be delivered by C-section if my life was determined to be at risk, fish would be viable but in the NICU for three to four months. Should I not need to be delivered at 24 weeks I would be admitted to the hospital, monitored, and kept on strict bed rest with the goal of reaching 34 weeks. Thank goodness, we found someone who believed in us. Someone who would fight for our baby, who would fight for us. We left with an appointment for the following week and relieved hearts.

The day before our next appointment, Faithyyy had a holiday concert at school and proudly wore her ugly sweater, wanting so badly to tell everyone she was going to be a big sister. That night, at the concert, at 7:02 p.m., we felt fish dance with little flutters for the first time. Either that or I was having gas from the tacos we ate for dinner. Who knows for sure, but I chose to go with a dancing fish over a mommy full of gas. First thing the next day we got the call that our fish was a girl and had straight A's on her first report card. Our fish became MaryGrace Hope as we headed in for our 12-week anatomy check for more A's. The tone of this visit was a bit different, though, as the doctor had a chance to look fully into ALL of my medical records. "Annette, you didn't tell me about what happened with your last pregnancy. The blood loss, transfusions, the HEART ATTACK. Why didn't you tell me?" The doctor stood there looking at me deeply. I responded, "1. It didn't come up and I knew you had my medical records, and 2. I was medically cleared and the heart attack was just because I lost five units of blood in an hour." I didn't do good things for my case. "A 42-year-old has a heart attack and also loses five units of blood from a first trimester pregnancy loss, it's not good. This makes me even more concerned for you and this pregnancy. I am not sure you are strong enough, physically, to carry this baby. I think we need to look into termination." Why were people so intent on taking MaryGrace away from me, away from us, away from her home? The doctor suggested that we try again in a few months, but we knew right away, even though we still had one embryo remaining, we would not try again. She went over all the risks with us, what to do if I started bleeding. She would want me to rent an apartment or something close to the hospital in about a month. She clearly understood we were not terminating.

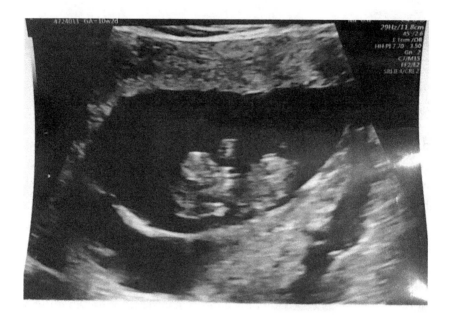

Christmas

The doctor suggested I gradually come off of bed rest and enjoy the holidays with my family, as the move to be by the hospital would likely happen in February and we would be separated from one another during the week unless all three of us moved. I was terrified. I had not bled since the spotting at our first OB appointment, and I still checked every hour to make sure. It was so important for our family to be together at Christmas Eve services, which meant all three of us. Tom and Faith had been going to church without me in the previous weeks, but we needed to be together to praise the birth of our King. I also knew I needed to pray really, really hard, and the best place to do that was in God's house. I held MaryGrace (via my belly) the entire service and I prayed like I have never prayed before. I prayed for the blessings I have been given, I prayed for repentance and redemption, I confessed my fears and my anger and then I thanked God because of his miracles, because He knows what it's like to lose a child, and He gave me comfort.

Christmas Eve excitement must have tired Faith out because she slept REALLY late on Christmas Day. At 10 a.m. and full of parent excitement, we woke Faith up with a "clatter," and she "sprung out of bed to see what's the matter." Experiencing Christmas Day through the eyes of a child has to be one of the top 10 lifetime joys. After Faith opened her last present, she stood up all lost and confused. "Faithyyy what's wrong?" I asked. She started to cry and said, "Santa didn't bring anything for MaryGrace...I got her this 'lil guy" —holding up a bear— "do you think she'll love it?" "Of course, she will love it as much as I love you." The rest of the day(s) seemed like a blur. In actions I was going through the holidays, but in mind and heart I was floating above it all, watching it happen but being paralyzed with fear. I was on "auto pilot." I was numb. Tom's dad, Big Tom, came to visit us for the holidays and arrived on Christmas Day evening. Tom picked Big Tom up from the airport and told him about MaryGrace on the way home. Big Tom was a very happy grandpa. He knew this was a miracle we had been praying for, for a very long time.

> **Backstory:** I had always wanted to make prime rib for Christmas dinner and this was the year I decided to do it. I would be gradually coming off of bed rest and felt we needed to have some sort of a celebration to enjoy the pregnancy. I bought a $125 prime rib and let it cook low and slow for the majority of the day. It was perfect. It was also a little too rare for Big Tom, so he decided that we could microwave it to cook it the rest of the way. In 10 minutes my beautiful rare-to-medium rare (depending on your definition) went medium well to beef jerky. Yes, that night we celebrated with $125 worth of beef jerky.

Now that Big Tom knew, it was time to tell the rest of the North Carolina family. Patti was a huge help in pulling off this surprise;

she had everyone over to her house to celebrate Christmas and we planned to call right after dinner. Tom called and everyone was on speaker phone. Tom said, "We have some news to share with 'y'all'. We are having a baby girl. MaryGrace will be here in June." Silence, silence. Jonathan was the first to speak up, and he was so surprised but also happy to have another sister but announced in advance that he was done with diapers. The rest of the family congratulated us too. We didn't hear from Bailey, but Jonathan told us she stepped outside to get some air. The news was something Bailey had not expected at all, and she was worried about having a relationship with another baby sister. Tom and I ended the call sad but very much in love with our growing family. Our love was strong enough to bring everyone together.

Through this all I was afraid that there was something wrong with MaryGrace, and I lived in denial, and even after losing Tommy I refused to think there was something wrong in my body. We listened to her heartbeat every night to make sure she was okay, and her heartbeat was also my lullaby and sounded like angels singing. It was the only way I could get a few hours of sleep. Faith loved to listen to and call MaryGrace on her cell phone (my belly button). She would pray with MaryGrace and tell her "Listen, MG, when I was in Mommy's condo, the same condo you are living in, things were kind of rough at first but I fought hard and kicked to always let everyone know I was good. I need you to do the same thing, MG, fight...fight like you ran out of cookies in the cabinet. If you fight and are born, then big sister will give you lots of cookies." Then Faith would turn to me and say, "Mama, don't worry. I had a talk with my little sister and she knows big sister is always right and means business. She's gonna be okay, Mama." And with that Faith would kiss us good night and tell her daddy, "You need to tuck me into bed, Daddy, it's getting late. Mommy needs her sleep and MaryGrace needs to think about our conversation, right MaryGrace?" Hey, who were the mom and dad? Sometimes the lines got a little blurred.

We told the world that we were pregnant on New Year's Eve. I was hesitant, but Tom reassured me that we should. This pregnancy may not be going the way we wanted, but we WOULD be having a healthy baby on June 1st, at the latest. We posted our 12-week ultrasound picture, the one where MaryGrace was making duck lips, and said, "We'll be popping a different type of bottle this year." With that, the congratulations and well wishes and heart emojis came flooding in. This didn't help my fear and sent my anxiety sky high, although I appreciated all the messages of love from across the United States.

Bailey flew in to see us on the third of January. At this point in my pregnancy I had a round baby belly, I was wearing maternity clothes, and it was quite obvious that I was pregnant. Bailey enjoyed listening to MaryGrace's heartbeat, too, and we created a bond and further celebrated that bond by doing each other's makeup. More like Faith doing our makeup and hair. We were "runway ready" … for bed.

We enjoyed a wonderful family breakfast together and took Faith to dance so she could work on her solo and duo for competition. Driving down the Pacific Coast Highway (PCH) I had a contraction and pressure between my legs and then another contraction. Of course, my mind went to the worst while Tom tried to help me remain calm and consider that it could just be Braxton Hicks or growing pains. I wasn't bleeding, the contractions stopped, and my water hadn't broken, so we convinced each other (at this point) that everything was fine. We ended a wonderful visit with Bailey at a baby store. I really wanted Bailey to be involved, feel involved, and know in her heart that she is loved. I asked Bailey and Faith to pick out the theme for the nursery and I would go with whatever the two big sisters decided as long as they worked together as a team. We left the store with a theme, MaryGrace's first bear, and a number of other essentials that brought the girls so much joy to pick out together. Yes, Tom did have another panic moment looking at the strollers...some things never change.

I had the countdown going on my phone waiting for the seventh, our next visit with the perinatologist and the next time I would see MaryGrace. On the way Tom and I discussed what we would do and say if the doctor brought up termination again, and we decided that we would no longer discuss it and shut the conversation down tight. Every fiber of my being was scared. I knew we were making the right decision for MaryGrace, but were we making the right decision for Jonathan, Bailey, and Faith? Was I making the right decision for my family? In preparation I had done some research about my life insurance and I made sure Tom knew, Big Tom knew, and I had it written down in my bedside table. We had to have the conversation, and Tom fought me on this every minute of the conversation, but he needed to know. He needed to know because I didn't have a will. He needed to know because he would need my life insurance to take care of the family. He had to know so that he could make decisions as my next of kin. He had to know, and I felt like I was yelling at him, "Listen to me! Listen to me. We can't make this decision without you listening!"

The medical assistant weighed me and I had only gained three pounds through the holidays! My oxygen level was good, but my blood pressure was up a bit at 135/80. Here is the only funny thing that happened at this appointment: the medical assistant said, "Your blood pressure is elevated. Are you stressed about anything? Are you worried about your visit?" Gee, just a bit! The doctor herself brought us back right away. She didn't waste any time, even after her medical assistant told us she was running an hour behind. The doctor did the ultrasound and MaryGrace was beautiful, still measuring 1.5-2 weeks ahead of her gestational age and laying on her tummy sucking her thumb, and her heartbeat was amazing at 128 BPM. They remarked that her head and feet were quite large, but we weren't surprised one bit. MaryGrace's lungs were developing on schedule, her spine was spectacular, she had two perfect kidneys, and she needed to poop. The doctor said she was beautiful and perfect and then proceeded to do a vaginal scan to check the areas of concern. The doctor stopped talking and continued to scan and take pictures for about 20 minutes, and when she was done, she simply said, "Get dressed and I'll be back so we can talk," left the room, and closed the door. It felt like forever until she came back in, and when she did, she turned on the lights and sat down. She pulled her stool up closer to me so she could hold my hand. "Annette, I think we have taken this pregnancy as far as we can, given your cardiac history. Your life is in danger. We need to terminate."

"No," I said, "we've talked about this."

"You can try again in a few months after your body has healed. We could try a D&C, keep you in the hospital, and monitor for bleeding. If no bleeding, you can have another baby."

"I don't want another baby. I want this baby. Why are you starting this again?"

Pause.

"The placenta has grown past the wall of your uterus. It has grown towards your kidneys, your bowel, and has now taken over 70% of your cervix, and there is a lot of blood flow in your cervix. We have taken this pregnancy as far as possible. If you start bleeding, we will not be able to save your life. The blood will come out faster than we can pump it into you, and your heart won't be able to take it."

"We won't have another baby. I cannot go through this heartbreak again. We have already lost five babies. MaryGrace will be the sixth. Faith's heart will be broken. Please. Please fix this."

"I can't," said the doctor.

"You can. You just don't want to fix it."

The doctor just looked at me and started to cry herself. "Annette, no doctor can fix this. If I could, I would."

"I want a second opinion." Seeing another doctor would actually be my third opinion.

"I will help you get in to see another doctor at another hospital."

Our appointment with the third perinatologist was that following Monday. A week seemed like forever. Every day I did my best to work and be a cheerful mommy for Faith. I cried a lot, I rubbed my pregnant belly and always kept at least one hand on my belly, and I prayed. I prayed with all my might. Listening to MaryGrace's heartbeat was so soothing, and we continued to do that every night. Hearing her heartbeat gave us strength and hope that perhaps she was healthy enough to stick with us through all of this. I didn't sleep. I didn't eat. I had never felt so scared and sad in my life. I cried to Tom to "fix this," I cried, "Fix this, fight for our baby," and he would cry back that he can't fix this, but he would fight with me. We did an internet search for doctors who were experts in treating pregnancies with placenta increta. We found one doctor at a different university hospital. Tom called, but the nurse would not make an appointment without a referral from our OB. Still fighting for our daughter, we did another internet search for that doctor's personal email address, and Tom emailed begging the doctor to help us. The doctor responded in agreement and made an appointment for two days after we would see the third opinion doctor; he had already set it up with his assistant. I just had to make it one week. Come on, MaryGrace, and fight with us. We felt optimistic.

Our appointment with the third opinion doctor was at 8:30 on a Monday morning. Tom and I headed out at 5:30 a.m. to deal with

LA traffic. I am so grateful that Big Tom continued to stay with us and said he would stay as long as we needed. Big Tom took over for us in the house and with Faith so we could fight for MaryGrace. The ultrasound technician came in first and said they had received all my medical records for this appointment. Panic set in. Don't give us the same outcome because you don't want to go against a peer. I stopped the ultrasound tech. "I want to see the doctor first." The doctor came in and introduced himself. The first thing I said was "If you cannot give an independent opinion of our daughter's outcome, then we can end this appointment right now." The third opinion doctor assured us that he would give his own assessment and then said, "But you are my patient. Your daughter is not, and my obligation is to your health. Do you understand?" I wanted to say no, but Tom said, "Yes, I understand for the both of us." At that moment I realized that if the doctors couldn't save the both of us, then Tom wanted me.

The ultrasound tech returned and did her scan. MaryGrace received an A+ on this scan, and we even saw her peeing. The tech gave us a picture of her very large foot and proceeded with the vaginal ultrasound. The room was silent, and the ultrasound tech did not look at me. When she was done, she simply removed the wand, handed me wipes, and said, "Get dressed and the doctor will come in to speak with you."

Our reproductive endocrinologist is truly amazing and was with us through it all. Even at this third opinion appointment, he adjusted his office appointments so he would be available to be on speaker phone while we spoke with the third opinion guy.

The doctor came in and did not smile. He sat down and we got our reproductive endocrinologist on the phone.

"Annette, I am sorry you had to wait so long. I emailed your scan images to all of the perinatologists in my group. We also had a quick call. This way I was able to check with each doctor to get their assessment and treatment plan."

"Oh wow, thank you!"

"Don't thank me yet. Annette, everyone is in agreement. It is not safe for you to continue this pregnancy. The placenta is less than one half of a centimeter from the tip of your cervix. We agree with your doctor that you need to terminate."

Our reproductive endocrinologist spoke. "We really need to save this baby. Can she be admitted until viability? Can you sew her cervix shut? There has to be an option."

I was numb and felt like I was in the room but floating above. All I heard were voices, not words, and during this time the two doctors were having a clinical discussion. I came back to reality and heard my RE say, "Oh, I see. Annette, I am so sorry. I agree with the doctors. You cannot continue this pregnancy." It felt like the world was against my daughter, and I was out of fight. I felt like I was in the midst of a nightmare with everyone trying to kill me and I just stood there, letting it happen.

The third opinion doctor said that I needed to terminate immediately. Given the placenta growth in six days, he estimated that I had one to two days until my condition became a life or death medical emergency.

"Fine, do it today."

"I can't. You will need a surgery team comprised of several specialties, one being an oncology gynecologist who is skilled at removing uteruses in this type of situation."

"Remove my uterus?"

"Yes, it will be the only way to save you."

"Please don't make me go home. My daughter is already in love with her baby sister, and she will want to hug and kiss my pregnant belly. Please don't put her through that."

"I will call your other doctor and have her set this up immediately." He looked at Tom and said, "Here is my number. If you do not hear from your other doctor by noon, call me." And as we left the office staff stopped in the halls, looked at us, and everyone said, "I am so sorry." The receptionist said, "I am so sorry. Don't worry about your co-pay. We will bill you."

The drive home was rough. We didn't talk. We both just cried. There were no words. We got home and Big Tom knew the outcome by the tears in our eyes. He hugged us both tight and started to cry himself. Tom and I went upstairs to lie in our bed and hold each other through the tears. The family planning clinic called right at noon. When terminating a pregnancy, you are no longer seen in a comfy doctor's office but are transferred to the brown old building on the back of the property, simply named "Family Planning." The chief of family planning had personally taken on my case. We were instructed to be in the office by 8 a.m. and also told that, if possible, they would do the surgery the same day. That evening when we told Faith, she knew something was wrong.

"Faith, MaryGrace has to go to heaven."

"Why, Mommy? I thought we were good now? I told all my friends I was going to be a big sister. Everyone knows," she said through heartbroken tears.

"Honey, I thought so too. But MaryGrace will be in heaven with her brothers and sisters and her grandparents. She will be in our hearts and we will see her again someday."

"Mommy, I want her here with us." Me too, Faith, me too!

I lay down with Faith to help her through her tears, and when she stopped crying, she said, "Mommy can I give her one last kiss?" and she did and hugged my belly. "MaryGrace, I will be okay. I am still your big sister. I love you, MG." The rest of the night she seemed fine, but I know she was being really brave. Nobody asked or wanted to hear the heartbeat that night.

Another 5 a.m. wake-up to head downtown in silence. This was seeming all too familiar. We walked into the old brown building that smelled as old as it looked. The only pictures on the way were posters of family planning options. As I sat waiting for the doctor, I was seeing the journey we had taken to get to where we were now. Two IUIs, four IVF procedures, three operations to correct fertility problems, six embryo transfers, ten years, $300k, millions of tears and a lot of broken hearts. I thought about all the tragedy our family had walked through because of me: four knee surgeries, a stroke, five miscarriages, sepsis, a car accident, a heart attack, and now this. I had brought so much hurt and pain into my family's life. I was bargaining with God, if I survived this surgery, then I will be the mom to Faith and wife to Tom that they deserve. I also felt an overwhelming need to go to heaven with MaryGrace so that I could take care of her and Tom and Faith could start over and build a new life without the sadness I had brought into our lives. Still waiting, I started to go over my life insurance, savings, IRA, etc. again so Tom knew what to do. He still did not want to hear any of it, but, again, I needed him to hear it.

The doctor called us back. The first doctor we would see was doing her fellowship studying with the chief of family planning. She sat down with us to do our pre-operative exam and have us sign the consents.

"Are we going to do this today?"

"No, I am sorry we are not. We need to reserve an operating room, the surgical team is clearing their schedules, it's just not possible today. This is a big surgery, and you will have about ten surgeons in with you." It was not fair, knowing we had to say goodbye to our baby girl. It was urgent that we do it but not too urgent. I was confused.

I started to cry and said, "Is there any chance to save the two of us, something that hasn't been discovered yet? Please, please save my baby!" The doctor lowered her head and looked at me, crying, "I wish there was. We don't want to do this any more than you do. But YOU are our patient, and we can't save the both of you."

I couldn't sign the consent for termination and surgery. I didn't want this at all. I refused to sign. The doctors at that point said I wasn't able to make critical decisions about my health and had Tom sign. Which I said was the best thing to do because had it been up to me, I would have gone home and come back June 1st.

"Annette, next I want to give you in an injection in your uterus that will stop blood flow in your uterus."

I replied, "What will happen to MaryGrace?"

The fellow responded, "Her heart will stop beating pretty quickly after the injection. We have to stop the blood flow so you do not bleed out before we start the surgery."

"You want me to go home, to my house, to my daughter, with my dead baby?"

"Yes, that would be the plan."

I started to yell and cry the hardest tears. "No! I won't do it. I won't go home with my baby girl dead in my womb. Admit me, do whatever, but I am not going home like this. I Do NOT want this!"

"Let me go check with my supervising physician."

After a long wait, both doctors came back into the tiny, smelly exam room. They made a plan and confirmed the surgery. "I have booked an OR for tomorrow at 1 p.m. Come into the hospital at 8:30 a.m. to get registered and admitted, and we will do the injection in the hospital no later than 9:30 a.m." The chief sat and held me while I cried for about 45 minutes.

They gave me a sleeping pill for that night, knowing that I wouldn't be able to sleep, and instructions for arranging for a funeral home to pick up MaryGrace's remains. I was at my absolute lowest. I felt like a martyr. We wanted this baby for a very long time, and Faith prayed for this sibling for over six years. After all the prayers, hopes, dreams, and medical procedures, we had a baby and I needed to terminate her life, choosing mine over hers, my life over an innocent baby's life.

We received the orders for lab work and before being sent to the main hospital to have my pre-op with the anesthesiologist and my blood work, but before they sent us over, the doctors handed us one last consent, a consent to release MaryGrace to a funeral home after she was "delivered." That was the final knife right in the heart: making funeral arrangements for our daughter, a daughter who would die because of my body and a choice that really wasn't a choice. On the way home we contacted the local funeral home and made arrangements for cremation for our daughter. I even picked out her urn.

On January 15th, 2020, we left for the hospital at 5:30 a.m. It was a hard drive with traffic and a sad drive knowing this would be the last few hours with MaryGrace alive in my womb. Tom was so distracted he nearly rear ended a truck. We arrived at the main hospital and held each other's hands tight, both crying as we walked through to registration and then down to the OR. The assistant at the main desk for pre-op didn't understand why were there so early before our OR time. I said, "My doctor wanted me to come early for a procedure before the surgery."

She replied, "What procedure?"

"My doctor has the details."

She became insistent. "WHAT procedure?"

I couldn't hold back and emotions came screaming out of my mouth. "I AM KILLING MY BABY TODAY!"

Her only reply was "I will have the charge nurse get you a bed."

The tears were flowing uncontrollably and I started hyperventilating. Tom and I, still holding each other's hands tightly, went to the pre-op waiting room, where we sat for two or three minutes before we were called back. Right at 9:30 a.m., both the fellow and chief came into my pre-op room. After the hi, hi, you doing okay—um no, banter, the fellow told me that after they do the injection, I may need to go sit back in the waiting room as some of the nurses were upset and against what we were doing, and those nurses wanted me out of pre-op while MaryGrace's heart stopped. I felt that same way, but why do they get a choice and I don't? This wasn't a decision based on not wanting our baby. I was assured that the chief was talking to the charge nurse to see if they could settle things down.

The chief did one last ultrasound so we could see MaryGrace and hear her heartbeat one last time. She was also able to get us a picture. MaryGrace was now measuring two to three weeks larger than her gestational age; she was a big, healthy girl. I was so distraught that I didn't remember this ultrasound or the sound of her heart. Tom and the doctors told me at my final post-op, and the pictures were in the bag I packed for the hospital. I did remember what happened next. The fellow and chief had a solution in a vial and several needles. They had me lay down and asked Tom to hold me and love on me through these next steps. The doctors loaded up one syringe and, with ultrasound guidance, injected it into my uterus but missed the spot needed. As I was screaming from the pain and begging them not to do this, the second needle was put in, and I was screaming louder in pain and begging the doctors to stop and let my baby live. Tom was crying with me, and with each scream his tears got harder. He declared his love over and over and was telling me how much he and Faith cannot live without me. The charge nurse came over and closed the sliding door of my pre-op room and stood out there as a guard. The final syringe went in and the doctors covered me up and simply walked out, fighting back tears. The charge nurse came in and told me I could stay in the room, but she also needed to start an IV, and I needed to take some oral medicine prior to the surgery which I threw up. I don't remember much of what happened after other than several nurses coming in one at a time to apologize, pray with, and hug us.

The next thing I remember was entering the OR surrounded by surgeons, residents, and interns. The room was full, and as I was wheeled in, they had formed lines on both sides of the gurney and each touched my hand gently, as if they were praying by touching me. I brought MaryGrace's hat in with me, and it was my desire to have MaryGrace wrapped in her hat so she wouldn't be cold and that her hat stay with her until cremation. The fellow came and sat with me. She told me that I needed to hold onto the hat tight and they would take it from my hand when it was time. She sat by my side, asking me questions about Faith, and as I answered with tears, the anesthesiologist injected medicine into my IV and I drifted off.

Backstory: When I first learned that MaryGrace would be born early, I had a custom hat made for her in preemie size with a matching blanket covered in rainbows. Both had her name so that everyone in the NICU would know her name and know how much she was loved.

I woke up in recovery late that evening with Tom sitting by my bedside. I was in the worst pain I had ever experienced physically and emotionally. I had IV catheters for blood in my hands, my shoulders, and my feet. The recovery room nurses wheeled me into my hospital room after midnight. I had come into the hospital that morning with a healthy pregnancy, and I was going to sleep empty.

Tom filled me in on what happened: I was in surgery for over four hours, Big Tom came to the hospital to sit with Tom, and after two hours the doctors had called in the waiting room and told Tom they were nearly halfway through with the surgery and that MaryGrace had been born asleep via C-section. After the surgery the fellow and chief came to the waiting room to speak with Tom. The doctors told Tom that the increta was much worse than they realized; had the pregnancy continued they would have had to remove one of my kidneys and possibly a piece of my bowel, and that was if I had lived long enough to get me into surgery, which they didn't think possible. I was dilated to two centimeters and the placenta had started coming out through my cervix. It was a miracle that I had not started bleeding before the surgery, and based on what they saw and what they operated on, it was no longer a question of "if" (I would have bled out and died), it was a matter of "when" (I would have bled out and died), which by evidence and estimate, would have been a matter of hours. The doctors left me with a ten-inch incision, including the C-section line, with staples and sutures, and they took my uterus and my cervix. They had to remove and reattach my bladder to avoid "upsetting" the placenta. Had the placenta been irritated, then I would have bled out and they would not have been able to save me.

The morning after the surgery the chief and fellow came to see me, did an exam, and then sat my bedside to see how I was doing emotionally and tried their best to reassure me that we did the right thing. They showed me the picture of my uterus filled with holes from the placenta. The chief had broken sterility after MaryGrace was delivered so she could wrap MaryGrace in her hat, and she had an OR tech come and take pictures for us, which the chief emailed to me to view when I was ready. Later that evening I did look at the pictures. MaryGrace was a baby. She had ears, eyes, long eyelashes. I saw her brain, her hip joints, her large feet and long fingers (just like my dad). All this time I was worried that there was something wrong with MaryGrace when she was great; it was my body that couldn't sustain the pregnancy. I stayed in the hospital for six long days. Six days of excruciating pain and crying. On our last day the fellow came in to sit with us; she reviewed every detail of the surgery with me to help me understand I did what was necessary, necessary for Faith and Tom. She made a memory box for MaryGrace; she printed the pictures, and she gave us an infant hospital outfit, hat, and blanket. It was a beautiful box. With that I was discharged and instructed to follow up in two weeks to have my staples removed and we drove home without our daughter, MaryGrace Hope.

CHAPTER 12

GRIEF, AND GRIEF IN A PANDEMIC

Grandma Beatrice

My father died when I was 12 and I had never thought it was possible to hurt as much as I did at that time. I couldn't possibly imagine ever feeling happy again, ever living life again. I wanted to die and I wanted to be with my dad in heaven.

My grandma was the only one who understood me. She was the only one that could see through to my heart and head at the same time. My daddy and my grandma were my best friends.

Grandma lost the love of her life to a heart attack in 1963. She never thought it was possible to hurt as much as she did. She couldn't possibly imagine ever feeling happy again, ever living life again. She wanted to die and be with her husband in heaven. She was now a single mother, raising a child in busy Los Angeles and had to find in her heart strength to move forward, not for her but for her daughter, Ruth Ann, who was nearly 15.

My grandma sat with me, held me, let me weep, helped me hit pillows, let me yell, and then made me a chocolate malt with bananas and sat me down to talk. Grandma wanted to explain grief to me in a way that nobody could; she wanted to explain it from her experience.

My grandma said to me:
"Grief is like spilling spaghetti on your favorite white blouse. You're devastated. You're thinking, how could this happen? My favorite blouse is ruined? I can never wear it again? So, you go to the sink and you try and wash it out. You rub and rub and rub harder, and you are sad, you are angry and try some more, but it's not coming out, and you cry some more. You think you can do without it and buy a new blouse, but no white shirt will do. So, you wash it some more. You take it to the dry cleaners. Maybe the dry cleaners should give it another try. Why can't the dry cleaners make this better? Over time, the spot fades and you have found a blue blouse that will do, but it will never be as good as your white blouse, yet you wear it and every time you do, you think of that white blouse. You take the white blouse out of the closet, every now and then, to see if it was just a dream, or if the spot was magically gone, and while it's faded even more, it's still there. You will never forget that white blouse. How could you, it was your favorite. You think about it every time you see a white blouse. While you will never forget your white blouse and the faded red stain, you have managed to live life and you will always keep the memory of the white blouse with you, always!"

So, I asked her what heaven was like. My grandma told me that Grandpa Max said to her, before he died, that he was going to heaven and was going to get settled, find their cloud, and call for her. My grandma remained true to her wedding vows for the 49 years between their calls to heaven. My grandma was convinced that he had found a girlfriend and that was why he didn't call for her. Grandma was angry and said when she got to heaven, she was going to give Grandpa Max two black eyes. In the September before my grandma's death she cried to me about missing her Max and again mentioned the two black eyes. I reminded Grandma that heaven was a place of peace and of the ways she helped me understand death and grief. Grandma looked at me and said, "You are right. You are the smartest girl I know, Netsy Lambchop. I need to find peace and make up with my husband." Grandma died that February (2012) at 91 years old.

My grandma said to me:
"When someone dies, they live eternity in heaven. They find the fluffiest white cloud, with the best view, and settle in. I am sure your dad got a motorcycle. He always wanted one and was never allowed to get it. So, he will get his motorcycle and it will sit on his cloud. Your dad wants to be every place with you all the time, but he also wants to be with your sister and your mom and his crazy mother, too, so...he is going to ride that motorcycle and fly his cloud to wherever he wants to be, wherever he is needed, and he will watch over you. That's really why he needs his motorcycle, to keep up with you. There will be times in your life when you will feel alone, abandoned, maybe even hopeless, but then you will feel a brush of wind, a tickle on your nose, a butterfly will do a fly-by, or maybe your toe will start to itch (weird) and it's in these moments when your dad drove his cloud over you and is there watching over you. You are never alone. You have your own personal angel, just like I do with my husband."

My grandma was the best.
Of course, this met with a lecture on prom night, five years later.

My grandma said to me:
"Your date is super hunky. Don't come home tonight. You need to stay out all night."

I came home at 5:30 a.m. (post-prom school activities) and my grandma said to me, "Why are you home? It's prom night. Live life. You should be out making love to your guy...I will cover with your mom." That's my grandma, the wisest, the coolest, and apparently a true romantic, but she was also radically opposed to the tattoos I got as an adult.

My Grief

We left the hospital, leaving our baby behind, and when we got home, Big Tom and Faith had dinner ready for us and the couch was made up for me. It was good to be home but so hard to "act as if I was good" in front of Faith. Since I was still having issues with my bladder and not able to walk or do activities of daily living on my own, Tom needed to help me use the bathroom, sitting me down on the toilet and physically lifting me off. The poor guy even needed to wipe for me for the first few days at home. Tom would "walk me" a few times a day in our backyard, around the pool, until I was able to resume strength to walk on my own, then he walked beside me, and eventually I was able to walk around the backyard by myself. Sleeping on the couch was easier for me physically because I was able to sit up. Sleeping on the couch also kept me from going upstairs, not just because stairs were hard, but also because I couldn't face my bedroom. I lay in my bed in that room for months trying to keep MaryGrace safe. The same room where I lost our Tommy, the same place where there were still blood stains in the carpet.

The funeral home called the day after I got home and asked if we would like to spend some time with MaryGrace before her cremation. Tom, Big Tom, and I went to the funeral home, and we were shown into a family suite where MaryGrace lay in a bassinet (similar to the one we bought her). She was in a swaddle, with letter blocks spelling out her name. I also brought her special blanket. Big Tom had to leave as it was really hard for him to see his grandchild this way. Tom and I stayed and held our baby wrapped in both blankets. We kissed her. We said goodbye. We prayed over her. I rocked MaryGrace. Leaving the funeral home, I got faint and both Toms had to get me into the car as it felt like my legs were jelly and everything in my belly was stretching from the force of my tears. We received her ashes and urn two weeks later and brought our daughter, MaryGrace Hope, home.

The doctors assured me that my milk would not come in, but it did. I was leaking milk all the time. The doctors wanted me to bind my boobs so that the milk would stop, but I couldn't do it. This was MaryGrace's milk, and I wanted to keep it as long as I could. It was also the last time that I would experience lactation. I would extract the milk and put some on a piece of paper towel so the milk would dry and I would have a remembrance of MaryGrace's milk forever.

The nights were the worst. Although Tom slept beside me on the couch, the house was quiet and dark and Tom would fall into a deep sleep, so it was just me and my thoughts. I was having abdominal muscle spasms, signaling those muscles were healing, but it felt like MaryGrace kicking. Other times I would wake Tom up to beg him to get our daughter back. I had convinced myself that she was alive and taken away but we could make it better, we could get her back if we promised God we would be good parents. The only way Tom could get my attention was to tearfully tell me she was in heaven and remind me how she went to heaven.

When I was able to walk, Tom would wake up to find me pacing in the living room, making lists of everything that needed to be done, ever. Making those lists kept me from thinking about my reality. Tom said I was talking so fast that he couldn't keep up with me, and I would make lists about everything from packing Faith's lunch for the next day to organizing Christmas decorations. I was lost in post-partum depression with post-traumatic stress disorder and anxiety. The doctors, trying to help, would add more and more meds until I couldn't feel (anything) anymore.

My mind became "mush." I didn't know the day of the week or the time, and occasionally I would forget Tom's name. I was in such a fog that Tom and I were no-shows to Faith's award assembly, and I cried so hard that I had hurt my daughter. I cannot even imagine what it was like for Faith to walk into the multi-purpose room at her school, go up to the stage, get her award, come down the stage, and not see her mommy and daddy. That night she got pizza for dinner and I got a wakeup call.

Big Tom went home four weeks after the surgery. He had stayed in total for seven weeks. When he left, the reality of our situation came crashing down. How would we take care of our family and our home with this much pain in our hearts? We were on our own and had no help. Each day, though, we managed. Together.

On the way to my final post-op appointment, Tom told me about the final ultrasound, which I had forgotten. I let Tom know that I felt abandoned when he did not walk with the OR team and he did not kiss me before surgery. He did both of these, but I had no memory of either. My heart blocked so much of that day to help the pain. At the post-op appointment, I asked the chief to tell me again what happened and tell me again that I had no choice. She stood up and said, "Annette, I am not going to tell you anymore. You need to believe what I have said to you since the day after surgery. My telling you over and over again is not going to help if you are not going to trust. It took so much strength to do what you did. All of your choices were taken away. You only had one choice, 1) die and leave your daughter without a mommy or 2) save yourself." She continued, "You found strength to do what was right for your family. Now keeping finding that strength daily. Can you do that for me?"

Yes, yes I can. God brought me back five times now, and there was a purpose for his actions. God's plan was for me to be the very best wife, stepmom, and mom I can be for my family. I just had to fight my way back, which nobody could do for me. This also included fighting my way back from an arthritis and fibromyalgia flare up. For ten years my symptoms had been masked, and the auto immune disease put into remission, due to the hormones from both fertility treatments and pregnancy. Suddenly, without the hormones I went into a flare and again needed physical help to work through it. I knew I was a person, a woman, a wife, and a mommy but still didn't know who I was to myself. For ten years, outside of being a person, a wife, a mommy, I was a woman trying to get pregnant. For TEN years! Who am I now without the option of having another baby, without all the fertility treatments? My identity was lost and I needed to find my strength to be ME!

Grief in a Pandemic

As my physical recovery was coming to a steady state, until the next surgery to repair my bladder, the world was hit with the COVID-19 pandemic, and I was placed in quarantine because of my autoimmune issues and recent surgery. Having inflammatory arthritis, which was being treated, at that time, with a low dose chemotherapy, my team of doctors decided it was best that I fully quarantine and not leave the house nor risk exposure by my family leaving the house.

I already felt isolated and ashamed. I couldn't talk to anyone because I had so much emotional pain and anger for the decision I made. Only now we were all isolated from life. Faith's school (building) closed for the remainder of the school year, and Faith was now learning in a new virtual classroom world, and Tom was working at home so he could look after the both of us. I went back to work from home; it was time. Now it was more important than ever to find my strength in the dark. My method of compartmentalizing the pain, keeping it from Faith, and letting it out only while she was at school and dance was no longer an option. Faith needed me, and I knew that Faith seeing her mommy on the outside the way her mommy felt on the inside would only cause her more pain. She would be "okay" if I was "okay." We were in a new normal that couldn't survive without a happy home environment. We needed to organize, plan, and be creative.

I didn't grieve my other miscarriages and losses. I was ashamed to grieve out loud. So, I kept my grief inside my heart. When I lost MaryGrace, my grief compounded, and my feelings overwhelmingly poured out for all six AND the embryos that did not stick. I needed permission to grieve, which I received from a support group. I needed permission to not be ashamed. With each one a piece of my heart died. The piece of my heart that was reserved for that child.

Grief is heart-wrenching. Grief during a pandemic is your worst nightmare stuck on replay.

"When we lose someone we love
we must learn not to live without them,
but to live with the love they left behind." ~ Anonymous

CHAPTER 13

I FOUND MY STRENGTH IN THE DARK

Some say "Fake it 'til you make it," but I choose to say "Feel it 'til you make it." "Faking it" takes away your authenticity and it takes away who you are and what you've felt at each stage of your goal.

For those of you who are afraid or ashamed or confused about your feelings, I give YOU permission to feel; however, please feel your feelings safely, and after you have felt your way through them, I empower you to find your dimmer switch, to see the light, to find your strength and throw your glitter into the world.

I meditate.
I do some form of yoga.
I pray.

Each day I wake up making the decision to live for the day.
Each day I wake up and make a conscious decision to choose joy.

I give myself daily affirmations until I no longer need to say that affirmation because I believe it in my heart. Wait! I promised honesty, and I don't break my promises. Each day I choose joy, but I am by no means perfect, and it is not uncommon for me to end a work day feeling angry, or frustrated with Faith because she was being a pre-tween, or irritated with Tom because he cleaned the kitchen but has no idea where he put the can opener (Tom, the can opener should go in the silverware drawer), or I am upset with myself for eating a brownie (ugh, why are they in the house anyway) or more often that I am feeling my way through the stages of grief. I have learned in all of this, though, to give myself grace and start each day not giving up on the choice to choose joy. More truth: I couldn't say my affirmations for the first few weeks, and because I made a commitment to myself (and to my family), I took out colorful pens and my journal and drew my affirmations, and prayers, every day until I could say them out loud.

"Today, I boldly make the decision to live life for today and will act with intention."
"Today, I boldly make the decision to live life for today and will act with intention. I believe in myself. Yesterday I took one breath at a time!"
"Today, I boldly make the decision to live life for today and will act with intention. My belief in myself and my abilities as a wife, mom, friend, and employee are stronger each day. For two days now, I took one breath at a time!"
I repeated this affirmation to myself for 31 days and each day I felt stronger, more capable. I grew in my belief, and I lived for one day at a time.
"Today I choose peace."

I had my last bladder surgery in July of 2020, and as I write, I am recovering from another large surgery. I have not yet been able to resume my exercise routine, and grief and COVID-19 made it so easy to not be active and throw the healthy eating handbook out the window. Truth card on the table, I have gained 40 pounds, and I am out of shape. With the exception of yoga, I cannot exercise for the next three months; however, I can take back my healthy lifestyle through choosing what goes in and on my body. Yes, I did fall off track. Yes, I will stop making excuses. Yes, I have taken back control of my life. Yes, I learned that if I cannot find something desirable to eat then I am eating for comfort and not for hunger.

After what I had been through, this last surgery was nothing. As the nurse was beating on my hand to find a vein for the IV, she asked me how I just sat there and didn't say anything. After my babies going to heaven, the multiple surgeries, after having IVs in my feet and shoulders and waking up with multiple IV sites for blood transfusions, her beating my hand was nothing because it was a matter of perspective for me. I now measure things in terms of perspective and have taught Faith to do the same. Losing MaryGrace was a furious tiger, COVID-19 was a wild elephant, one last surgery was a chicken, and not being able to exercise for three months is a pygmy goat.

I love the ocean; it is where I find peace, it is where I find answers to questions I didn't realize I had, it is a place where I can be still and a place where I feel my strength. I often wondered why the ocean was "my place," and in the stillness of one day, after playing with Faith at the beach, the answer came to me. The ocean cycles its strength, just like I do. During high tide it is recharged and strong, and at low tide its strength ebbs as it pulls away. If the ocean is not expected to be strong all the time then why should I?

I have learned a few things along the way:

1. *Believe in yourself*—nobody holds the power to take your belief from you, and it's also nobody's responsibility to MAKE you believe in yourself. However, when you can't believe in yourself, then you can borrow belief elsewhere. Borrow the belief from a friend, spouse, child, the Bible, wherever, just don't stop believing, and when your belief is strong, pay the belief forward.

2. Nobody can MAKE you feel. You are responsible for your own feelings.

3. "Yes, Yes, I Can." – Yes, yes, YOU can!

4. It is okay to feel the feelings YOU choose.

5. It is okay if you are not strong every hour, every minute of every day.

6. It is okay to go through your day one breath at a time, as long as you do not stop breathing.

"If we climb over our troubles, if we dance upon our fears, if we patch up our world, we will laugh away our tears, and we will find the strength to stand tall, oh and then, we'll have it all. Life can be so unfair, but I swear our future's bright, that's why I write to you, sending these words of hope, with the warmest hug, inside an envelope.
So read this if you would, and maybe, just maybe, we can try again."
"Hug Inside An Envelope" - performed by Jeff Pike
Lyric by Rosalind Winton, music by Robert Benson

AFTERWORD

Thank you for following my journey to find my strength. It is important to share my journey because I believe that many of us find ourselves in similar places at different points in our lives. If, by sharing my journey, I have helped or inspired at least one of you to find your strength, then this has all been worth it. If not, I hope you took comfort in knowing of my transformation.

My journey is not done yet because I boldly continue my journey with intention, and with a strength and belief unlike any other.

THANK YOU

Froggy Bear, for believing in me unconditionally, loving me with all my faults (perfections), and fully supporting my goat onesie. I love you, truly, always and forever.

Jonathan and Bailey, thank you for adopting me into your lives and allowing me to be a bonus mom to you both, otherwise said, your Netsy. I am so very proud of you and grateful every day for the blessings you experience in life and the way you both live life without fear or regret. Keep reaching for the stars, Snickerdoodle and Bailey-Pie. There is no obstacle you cannot overcome.

Faithyyy, you are the only one that knows me from the inside out. You are a constant reminder that anything is possible. You are my greatest blessing. You will always be my baby Foofy, I will forever be your mommy.

To all of our heavenly babies who have reminded me of God's greatest vision.

To those who will and will not read my book.

To my mother, Ruth, and stepfather, Marc, your belief and love have encouraged me to make my dream a reality.

To my Southern in-laws for making Tommy.

To Rosalind Winton and Jeff Pike whose words speak to my soul. Thank you for making music that touches lives

To my wonderful photographer Jacklin Fraser for giving me sexy legs.

To my heavenly friend Andy for getting the bums out of my life.

To "Jake" for being a constant friend and letting me share our story.

BONUS

Jeff Pike - Hug Inside An Envelope
A Song of Hope and Reconciliation.

Lyric by Rosalind Winton
Music by Robert Benson

For more information on Jeff Pike visit - www.JeffPike.com
www.linktr.ee/jeffreypike

For information on Rosalind Winton visit - onevoiceliteraryagency.
com/my-music

To download your copy of "Hug Inside An Envelope" scan the QR
code below.

ANNETTE PEARSON

has had a passion to write and share her story from a very young age. Annette felt that her life resembled a com-drama, so she kept a very detailed journal as if that journal was her book. Annette's dream is now a reality with her first book, '*Finding Strength In The Dark*', and those detailed journals will be published in January 2021.

Annette's story began when her parents divorced at the age of four. As Annette got older she became very independent but yet made poor decisions in relationships. Annette survived a physically and sexually abusive relationship knowing that the only way out was to sleep/live in her car. As life continued Annette powered through four knee surgeries including a total knee replacement, a car accident where she was severely injured, six miscarriages, and an autoimmune disease. Annette proudly declares that she is a survivor, a warrior, a champion, and it all began with taking the first literal step and affirmation.

Often people ask Annette, 'how are you still walking, talking and smiling, how do you do it?' and Annette's response is always "because I choose to do so." Annette encourages others through influence and affirmations to live life for themselves, to find their inner warrior and wear it proud. Annette shares her journey in a raw and real way that engages the audience with her honesty and insights while adding a light touch of sarcasm and humor because Annette also considers laughter a form of meditation. Annette's goal for writing this book is to be able to help women find their strength, too. She shares a message of hope, love and faith.

Annette shared her story in a support group she attended after her daughter was born asleep in January 2020. She now pays that support forward by helping women through social media platforms and her blog. Annette will be speaking to groups about her experiences, feelings and her reality, while finding the strength to deal with life's challenges. Annette is passionate about sharing her message so that all women know they do have the strength, they just need to look inside and turn their dimmer switch on.

Annette Pearson is a wife to Tom, a mother to Faith, a bonus mother to Jonathan and Bailey, and a mother to her six heavenly babies.

Annette is available to speak to support groups, organizations and schools, on:

Finding the strength to keep going

- How to tell your story
- Finding your tribe
- Taking one step at a time

Finding the joy in the life that has been forever changed

- Identify your 'what now'
- Knowing your purpose
- It is not your fault and you are not alone

Tools to help us find and keep our strength

- The importance of laughter
- Your journey of growth through affirmations
- Taking the first steps in healing by using your personal tool box and dimmer switch

Contact Annette at **Annette@Igotfaithbaby.com** to inquire about her speaking at your event, availability and rates. Annette will often speak to non-profits free of charge and offers 1 on 1 coaching sessions. Annette is available for virtual and in person speaking engagements.

ABOUT THE AUTHOR

Writing a book has been on Annette's bucket list since before bucket lists were cool. Eventually Annette's dream became a reality with her first book, *Finding Strength in the Dark*. When not working or writing books and her blog, *I Got Faith Baby.com*, Annette can be found taking care of her family, in the car with her husband Tom driving back and forth to her daughter's dance school, making family schedules, soaking in the hot tub, and influencing a healthy lifestyle. Annette currently resides in Simi Valley, California with her husband, Tom, daughter, Faith, and two dogs, Toby Jr. and Billy Jo No No. Annette also is a stepmother of two wonderful (now) adults, Jonathan (26) and Bailey (20), who live in North Carolina. Living in California is perfect for Annette as she makes an effort to get a minimum of ten minutes a day in the sun, which she refers to as "recharging solar cells." In addition to facing infertility challenges, Annette is a warrior, living life with inflammatory arthritis, fibromyalgia, and reactive leukocytosis.

CPSIA information can be obtained
at www.ICGtesting.com
Printed in the USA
FSHW021943240121
77968FS

9 781922 497246